Beyond Blame

Beyond Blame

A New Way of
Resolving Conflicts
in Relationships

Jeffrey A. Kottler

Jossey-Bass Publishers • San Francisco

Substantial discounts on bulk quantities of Jossey-Bass books are available to corporations, professional associations, and other organizations. For details and discount information, contact the special sales department at Jossey-Bass Inc., Publishers. (415) 433-1740; Fax (415) 433-0499.

For sales outside the United States, contact Maxwell Macmillan International Publishing Group, 866 Third Avenue, New York, New York 10022.

Manufactured in the United States of America. Nearly all Jossey-Bass books and jackets are printed on recycled paper that contains at least 50 percent recycled waste, including 10 percent postconsumer waste. Many of our materials are also printed with vegetable-based ink; during the printing process these inks emit fewer volatile organic compounds (VOCs) than petroleum-based inks. VOCs contribute to the formation of smog.

Library of Congress Cataloging-in-Publication Data

Kottler, Jeffrey A.
 Beyond blame : a new way of resolving conflicts in relationships / Jeffrey A. Kottler. — 1st ed.
  p. cm. — (The Jossey-Bass social and behavioral science series)
 Includes bibliographical references.
 ISBN 1–55542–604–2 (alk. paper)
 1. Interpersonal conflict. 2. Blame. I. Title. II. Series.
BF637.I48K68   1994
158'.2—dc20   93–35602
                                                   CIP

FIRST EDITION
HB Printing   10 9 8 7 6 5 4 3 2 1   Code 9408

The
Jossey-Bass
Social and Behavioral
Science Series

Contents

INTRODUCTION:
A Personal Journey Through Conflict 1

ONE
Identifying What Sets You Off 21

TWO
Exploring the Origins and Causes of Your Conflicts 39

THREE
Allowing Yourself the Discomfort 59

FOUR
Taking Responsibility Without Blaming 77

FIVE
Committing Yourself to Act Differently 101

SIX
Experimenting with Alternative Strategies 121

SEVEN
The Positive Functions of Conflict 147

EIGHT
Conflicts in Love 163

NINE
Conflicts at Work 185

TEN
When Conflicts Can't Be Resolved 205

About the Author 231

Recommended Reading 233

Beyond Blame

A Personal Journey Through Conflict

IT IS LATE AT NIGHT. I cannot sleep. Every time I close my eyes, I see before me a scene in which I stand helpless, mute, unable to express myself. I think of several things I could have said, brilliant responses that would have moved my adversary to tears, speechlessness, or, better yet, recognition that I am right and he is wrong.

In my dreams I can say these things, but I cannot seem to mobilize such persuasive arguments in the midst of real conflicts. "Why must he treat me this way?" I beseech the sandman, who will not release me from consciousness. "Why will he not be more reasonable, more cooperative, *more like me?*"

My breathing slows. I finally find a comfortable position. The demons are buried in sand and I am floating away. Suddenly, my eyes pop open once again. "Now, wait a minute," I remind myself. "Did he really mean it when he said . . . ?" "Next time he does that I am going to . . . " Indignation. Rage. Shame. Frustration. Fear. Tension. Uncertainty. Blame. No wonder I cannot sleep.

Even Experts Lose Control

I am an expert in human relationships. I resolve disputes for a living. I mediate conflicts, cool down hostilities between spouses, business partners, siblings, parents and children. I am a therapist, a trainer and supervisor of therapists. I have written a dozen books on how to do therapy. So it is with particular reluctance that I admit the extent to which I have allowed myself to become deeply troubled about relationships that have caused me great anguish and frustration. Furthermore, I cannot think of a time when this has not been the case.

I bring this to your attention not to perpetuate the myth (and it *is* an exaggeration) that most therapists are crazier than their clients, but to make the point that even with the best possible training and decades of experience helping others resolve disputes in their lives, everyone loses sleep over relationships in conflict.

I felt driven to figure out why interpersonal conflicts are unavoidable, why they occupy such a disproportionate amount of my time—thinking about them, reliving the most painful moments, obsessing about things I wish I had said or done, deciding who is most to blame, resolving to do better next time, and, worst of all, berating myself because, after all, I am the expert, and I should be beyond such mortal frustration.

In my search for answers to these questions I encountered a lot of reassurance from colleagues and authors of books on the subject. "Conflict is constructive," I read repeatedly. "Don't worry. You are not alone." I heard echoes of these sentiments from concerned friends. Yet this advice, however well meant, only contributed to greater feelings of impotence. This was true for more specific suggestions as well—to be more assertive, more firm, more flexible; to ignore the offending person's behavior; to not take the conflict so seriously. All of these simple platitudes are things I have heard myself say to clients a thousand times.

After studying the literature on human conflict in anthropology, ethnology, psychology, sociology, and political science, after interviewing several thousand people about their experiences during interpersonal disputes, I have learned that the key is not found in getting people to treat me differently. Neither is it in changing the way I respond to provocation, nor removing myself from threatening predicaments. And I now know that figuring out what is wrong with others, identifying why they behave so differently from the way I would prefer, defining the ways they are responsible for my suffering, is somewhat interesting but not all that useful.

Looking Inward Rather Than Outward

The thread that runs throughout almost all of my conflicts with others is the tendency to concentrate on the other person's role in obstructing my goals. The focus of most of my energy is on trying to place blame on other people, or on things outside of my control, rather than addressing what I am doing, or could be doing, to resolve disputes and reach my stated objectives.

This knowledge did not come easily; it took the forceful courage of one longtime colleague and friend, who pointed out a familiarity in my complaints about a particular person. Had there not been other times in my adult life in which I had been locked in conflict with someone who resembled the current antagonist? And was I not reacting in much the same way in which I had responded to others in the past?

These questions were liberating! Perhaps I no longer had to feel like the victim of unfair treatment. Maybe I could change the very fabric of my relationships, just as I purport to help others to do. If I could just get to the bottom of what is most disturbing to me, neutralize its effects, and move on to the things in life that matter the most! Indeed, this is exactly the path that I followed, one that is very familiar to me in my work with others, and one that helped me move beyond blame in order to focus on what is within my power to control.

Once I was able to stop holding another person responsible for my suffering, no matter how insensitively or manipulatively he acted, I was able to focus attention on my own role in the conflict. What is it about him that I find so threatening? How is it that he is able to get under my skin so easily? Why do I feel so sorely wounded by a person who really is not all that important to me?

I acknowledged my responsibility in seeking out not only characters who would disappoint me and withhold approval, but also those whom I could blame afterward for making aspects of my life less than satisfactory. Since there is certainly no shortage of people in the world who revel in trying to satisfy their need for power and control, I would always be able to find another candidate to victimize me. With this realization, my anger and indignation suddenly turned into disgust at myself. When was I ever going to learn? Was I doomed to spend my life struggling with the same core issues over and over again?

My personal journey through conflict went back through time. I began to look at the patterns of my life—By whom had I felt most rejected? In which relationships had I felt most be-

4

littled and helpless? I was able to conjure up images of all the people with whom I had had significant conflicts—from the first-grade teacher who had terrorized me with the claim that she could always see everything I was doing to a professional mentor who had ended our relationship abruptly without explanation. I visualized a gathering of these folks, perhaps a dozen of them together, sharing their frustrations in trying to deal with me. They offered one another sympathy and agreed that I deserved exactly what I had gotten.

It occurred to me that if such a convention of the antagonists in my life did take place, there probably would be remarkable consensus about what I am like. They would say I am too sensitive and thin skinned. I am too impulsive; I don't think before I open my mouth. There is something about me that is threatening to them.

Whether I agreed with this assessment or not, I was now well on my way through the *inner* journey of conflict. The problems that I was experiencing—and had repeatedly encountered before— were not just the result of people being difficult; nor were they only the consequence of miscommunication or interactive effects in some relationships. Every conflict is played out on a stage populated by others in the present. But just as importantly, these conflicts are re-enactments of previous struggles as well as depictions of events as we imagine them to be. Naturally, there is a lot of room for distortion and misinterpretation.

Finding the Patterns of Conflicted Relationships

In my efforts to understand and work through the conflicts of my life I have consulted many colleagues, supervisors, therapists, and friends. I have read virtually every book I could find on

5

the subject. I sought help from my adversaries, asked them about what I was doing that triggered their overreactions. I tried many different conflict resolution strategies, most with short-lived results.

Because of my fascination with the topic of conflict in relationships, I developed an expertise in working with difficult clients in therapy. I was determined to face what I most fear. This resulted in a book for therapists, a collection of research articles in a professional journal, and a series of workshops for professionals throughout North America and New Zealand.

While this knowledge and experience were certainly helpful in understanding the dynamics of what goes wrong in some relationships, what finally made the greatest difference for me was letting go of my demands that others change to be more like me. There is no use in blaming someone because he chooses to operate under rules that differ from mine. I can make decisions about how I interact with him in the future. I can feel like a victim and wallow in sympathy from others and pity from myself. Or I can turn away from my preoccupation with what others are doing or not doing and instead concentrate on resolving issues from my own past, putting these insights to work in such a way that I commit myself to act differently in the future.

I have been down this road with enough people—children fighting with their parents; siblings who will not speak to one another; spouses on the verge of divorce; friends estranged from one another; people in conflict with supervisors, co-workers, ex-spouses, neighbors—to know that there are few undertakings as difficult as coming to terms with conflict, both with others and within oneself.

6

What This Book Will and Will Not Do

You may have certain expectations about what a book such as this should do for you. A magical cure would be nice, but you are probably sufficiently familiar with this genre to limit your hopes to learning a few "techniques" or "strategies" that might make your life a little easier.

It has become fashionable of late to reduce complex human phenomena to a few simple premises that can be distilled further into several sequential steps to overcome most any problem. Thus whether you are interested in losing weight, stopping smoking, ending an abusive relationship, recovering from the ending of a good relationship, finding a better job, overcoming depression, reducing stress, conquering addictions, breaking bad habits, overcoming procrastination, finding love, or resolving conflicts, there are thousands of self-help manuals available that give you the steps to follow in order to achieve perfect harmony with yourself and all the universe.

And there is no scarcity of advice and guidance about how to deal with relationships in conflict. Some experts will tell you to learn negotiation skills, or the art of confrontation, or how to get others to do your bidding, or even the strategies of waging war. There are literally hundreds of plans that you might consult as a blueprint for neutralizing hostile actions.

Before I realized that the process of working through interpersonal conflict is more internal than external, I attempted to integrate what experts in the field of conflict resolution consider most crucial. Such a generic program includes several sequential steps, all sound advice if one's goal is to focus exclusively on changing other people's behavior.

1. *Create an optimal atmosphere for negotiation.* This includes providing a setting that is free from distractions and intrusions, one in which an attitude of cooperation rather than competition prevails. Both parties involved in the conflict feel safe enough to experiment, flexible enough to compromise.

2. *Describe the nature of the conflict from all perspectives.* Until a complete picture is created of what a dispute is about, it is impossible to address grievances. This means eliciting personal points of view from both people as to how they experience what is happening.

3. *Understand the behavior of your adversary.* Empathy is part of the picture—that is, imagining what the other person is experiencing, why he or she may be defensive or hostile or uncooperative. Equally important is understanding the context of the person's behavior. Is this a chronic pattern of obstruction, or is it specific to interactions with you? Is this person reacting to fear and stress, or is there some perverse hidden agenda operating? Figuring out the other person's motives and intentions is crucial to finding a means to resolve the dispute, or at least a way to protect yourself from further damage.

4. *Identify historical issues that may be involved in the struggle.* People argue not only about what is going on in the present but about what has happened previously. It is crucial to bring into the open unresolved issues, perceived injustices, and underlying feelings of resentment that have been lingering beneath the surface. This strategy is considered constructive only when the past is

brought in in an effort to understand the present rather than to rehash old fights.

5. *Declare needs that are not currently being met.* When each person takes responsibility for articulating his or her own issues, interests, needs, and feelings, effort is expended on finding solutions rather than excuses.

6. *Share decision making equally.* Resentment often stems from the belief that other people are controlling your life and dictating the terms under which you must function. When you feel that you are being manipulated or dominated by someone else, you harbor continuing resentments that affect your interactions. Most of this lingering hostility is diffused when the conflict participants make an effort to decide together what will be done.

7. *Develop alternatives that will meet stated goals.* If you are operating flexibly and negotiating from a position of compassion and strength, eventually you will find some solution that is satisfactory. This presumes that you are patient, that you have moved beyond finding fault or assigning blame, and that you are working together as a team to develop options that are acceptable to both of you.

8. *Initiate action designed to meet mutual goals.* Deciding on what you will do and how you will do it are certainly important steps. However, unless you have committed yourselves to some plan of action, all the good intentions in the world are meaningless. During this stage in the process each person declares what he or she will do differently in the future and what will happen if he or she does not follow through on this commitment.

9. *Reach a consensus on future actions*. An important theme running through this book is that conflict can be the most constructive or destructive of human interactions. It is not enough simply to resolve a particular dispute. The important thing is to learn from this exchange so that future interactions will be more caring and helpful.

Following the steps in this process is certainly a good idea. In fact, this is a *great* plan—as far as it goes. But in order to deal with conflicts in life, it is first necessary to move beyond blame. This includes bringing under control the indignation you feel toward others who do not treat you the way you expect; it also involves accepting that although you share responsibility for interpersonal disagreements, there is little to be served by blaming yourself for the difficult situations in which you find yourself.

What Is Unique About This Book?

This book has several unique aspects:

1. It is integrative in orientation, combining theory and research from diverse fields with a clinician's pragmatic concerns for helping people make a difference in their lives.
2. There is a focus throughout the book on taking responsibility for conflicts rather than blaming others for one's troubles. Attributing the causes of suffering to others may lead to short-term relief while creating escalating conflicts and producing long-term damage.
3. Some books are primarily insight oriented *or* action focused; this book is both. It helps counteract the tendency

to put conflicts "out there," and instead brings them inside, where something can be done about them.

4. Since attention is moved away from deciding who is at fault for conflicts, here emphasis is placed instead on what one can *do*, both inside his or her own head and outside in the middle of disputes, to respond more effectively.

5. No matter how patient, reasonable, and skilled one may be, he or she still will encounter others who do not operate by the same rules of conduct. This book explores why some people appear so difficult and why they fail to live up to our expectations for what we consider appropriate behavior. It examines why some people attempt to control others, and how blaming them for their behavior only makes things worse.

6. Whereas other works concentrate on conflicts within marriages or partnerships or friendships or with supervisors or between children and parents, this book takes a look at what all of these relationships have in common.

The Book's Process

Beyond Blame follows a process that is not unlike that of psychotherapy or any systematic learning endeavor. First it helps you assess what it is that you find most disturbing and disruptive. Next, you are helped to understand how these problems developed, what other issues they are related to, and how they are connected to lifelong patterns of avoiding responsibility and blaming things and people outside your control.

The book explores some of the unconscious forces at work that maintain continued self-defeating behaviors in conflict

11

situations. This may include an inclination to avoid confrontation whenever possible, indulge in the victim role for sympathy, or take some perverse pleasure from being able to blame others for your suffering. If you can assume you're not at fault, then you do not have to invest the hard work that is involved in changing. Instead you may complain that life has dealt you a bad hand, that you have had a string of bad luck, that you have not been treated fairly, that you are unappreciated by others.

Then it is decision time. Are you willing to pay the price to move beyond blame? Yes, you say tentatively, not altogether sure what you are committing yourself to. Caution is certainly appropriate under the circumstances: if you no longer choose to blame others for your conflicts and subsequent misery, then what is left is the realization not that you are at fault, but that you are responsible. This feels both burdening and exhilarating. On the one hand, you have nobody but yourself to blame when things are not going the way you would like. On the other hand, it is within your power to alter the course that conflicts are taking, even without the other person's consent or cooperation.

How this is accomplished is relatively less important than the determination to make it happen. It is not so much a matter of technique as it is an attitude—a willingness to keep trying different strategies until you get the results you want. Even when conflicts are irreconcilable, you still have options concerning how you will live with the predicament.

Clients in therapy are often frustrated because they want and expect easy answers, even though they know that is highly unlikely. Anything in life that is really worth doing involves work, usually with few shortcuts. The change process presented in this book is not a passive one. You can't just thumb through pages, reading words, nodding to yourself when you encounter

things you like and then moving on to the next book. In order
for significant change to take place in your conflicted relationships and in the ways you handle them, you will have to respond
actively to what you read. Specifically, this involves several
activities.

1. *Read carefully and critically*. Take notes. Talk to yourself.
   Argue with me when you disagree. Don't fight me—
   wrestle with the ideas. Discard what does not fit for
   you, but not before considering its possible validity.
   When an idea is particularly threatening, ask yourself
   why. Write about your reactions in a journal.
2. *Connect new ideas to what you already understand*. Make
   this material fit into your life, your values and attitudes,
   your unique situation. If you consider the spiritual, emotional, life-style, and philosophical influences that guide
   your life, you can appreciate the work you will need to do.
3. *Talk with others about what you are reading*. In order to
   make new ideas part of you, use them in your daily
   interactions with others. By now you probably have
   already been stimulated by a few things that have been
   mentioned here. Ask others what they think about
   these matters. Conduct your own research studies to
   confirm or refute what you have read.
4. *Practice*. Thinking and talking are fine, but without
   action on your part, you will remain nothing more than
   an enlightened but miserable wreck. Try out new ways
   of dealing with others. Experiment with what it is like
   to move beyond blame. Note the parts you like and
   those you do not. Change the way you define yourself,
   and others will soon follow.

13

The Process in Action

Beyond Blame is organized around a process of understanding and working through conflict that follows a series of progressive steps. Each chapter builds on the awarenesses and commitments developed in the previous sections and helps you internalize new concepts and apply what you have learned to specific conflicted relationships.

Let us look at an example of how this process might be applied. Nat was a person whose rage had gotten him in trouble so often that he landed in my office by court order: either he had to bring himself under control or he would end up in jail for provoking fights. This was a man who thrived on conflict as the nutrient that energized him through the day and well into the night. Yet he was utterly at a loss as to how he ended up in conflict with others so often—at work, at home with his children, even in restaurants and at parties. If there was a fight somewhere, he would always find himself in the middle of it.

Nat was actually quite an engaging and charming fellow. However, his anger was easily aroused. He might be involved in a most satisfying exchange with someone when all of sudden some button would get pushed and he would launch into offensive, aggressive behavior. He was being completely honest when he said that he had no idea what was triggering these reactions.

How was Nat ever going to identify unresolved issues that were so deeply buried in his unconscious? Three years of psychoanalysis was not the only solution. Another was the process that Nat went through with the assistance of a professional guide. That is the same path that you must take if you are ever to get beyond blame, control how you react in conflict situa-

14

tions, and respond in strategic, effective ways. Here is the process to follow:

1. Identifying What Sets You Off

People close to you have been telling you about it your whole life when you overreact to situations, exaggerate your victim role, and respond to situations in obviously self-defeating ways. For Nat, this took the form of feeling challenged by any man whom he perceived as functioning in an authority role. Usually such "trigger objects" appeared unusually confident and competent, perhaps even arrogant. Contact with these people signaled a reaction in Nat in which he had to cut them down to size, to take them on—if not verbally, then physically. Always in this scenario, Nat would tell himself that they were provoking him, that he had no choice but to defend himself.

Likewise in your own life, certain kinds of people and particular situations set you off in such a way that you lose control. These stimuli seem to elicit almost automatic reactions in you—unfortunately those in which you may exaggerate or distort what is happening and then overreact both in the ways you interpret what is going on and in the means by which you respond to it.

It is crucial that you recognize the consistent patterns with which you respond to others if you are ever to understand what is going on and then be able to do something about it. Once you have determined the possible sources of your reactions, the hard part is to use this self-knowledge to promote action rather than inertia. Insight may as easily be used as an excuse for avoiding action as it may be employed as an impetus for initiating change. You have known people who have been in therapy for years, who understand all too well why they are so dysfunctional, yet still persist in the same patterns. Self-understanding is nice, but unless insight is converted into action, it can sabotage efforts to change.

2. Exploring the Origins and Causes of Your Conflicts

You act in certain ways because you have learned to protect yourself from future harm based on past traumas. Once you have identified when you tend to overreact—who gets to you and what specific situations you dread—you will next want to figure out how this pattern evolved.

This stage was easy for Nat (especially with me pushing) since he could readily see how the people he fought with were mostly reincarnations of his abusive father. As a child he had felt powerless to oppose his father's will, but now as an adult he was determined to take on anyone crossing his path who was perceived as controlling.

3. Allowing Yourself the Discomfort

My primary purpose in the preceding stages was to turn up the heat a bit, to get in your face and ask you to look at the blame you direct outside of yourself for things that have not gone your way. If you noticed yourself feeling defensive, perhaps even a little angry at me for not understanding how difficult it has been for you, then you are in the middle of this next stage in the process.

When you notice yourself engaging in chronically ineffective behavior, when this pattern has been brought to your attention, it becomes more difficult for you to continue it and remain oblivious to the implications and consequences. Forever after, an annoying whisper will haunt you: "Look, you are doing it again. Blame others all you want, but it is *your* choice to continue this pattern."

When Nat picked an argument with me one day, rather than get into conflict with him, I took a step back and pointed out that I thought he was afraid of his feelings for me, that he was starting to trust me and value our time together. He could not tolerate the power he perceived I had over him: if he liked me, then I could hurt him. He protected himself by starting a fight in order to prove to himself that I was just a jerk like everyone else. When I brought this pattern to his attention, as he later learned to do for himself, he tried to hide an inadvertent smile of acknowledgment. He claimed this exchange "ruined" him: "It's just no fun picking fights anymore, Doc. Once I realize what I am doing—taking on my father, inflating my own power, avoiding a closeness with other men—I just don't have my heart in it anymore."

This is an example of insight at its best: when a realization about the way you behave creates sufficient dissonance that you have to change in order to feel comfortable again. If I tell you that the reason you blame others for your misery is because you do not want to take the responsibility for making things different, *and you believe me,* the next time you attempt this defense it will not work as well for you. You will hear my words, in your own internal voice, say, "Don't kid yourself! It is not *their* fault. What did *you* do that you might try doing differently?"

4. Taking Responsibility Without Blaming

As you know by now, the theme of this book is choosing to move beyond blame—toward others and yourself—and instead concentrate on what you can do to alter the situation.

Nat lamented his predicament, "How can I ever change this lifelong pattern, especially when others keep trying to push me all the time?" He had a lengthy list of all the techniques he had tried that had not worked for him: counting to ten before responding, taking deep breaths, using "I" rather than "you" as the pronoun of choice—all valid ideas. Rather than focusing on how others and the world were not cooperating with his new intention to act differently, we narrowed attention to what was within his power to control. He had choices about the extent to which he would allow other people to provoke him, and he had many options other than fighting as ways to respond.

5. Committing Yourself to Act Differently

It is one thing to muse about how nice it would be if only things were different; it is quite another to make a commitment to function differently in the future. After all, you have made thousands of promises to yourself—to lose weight, to get a better job, to stop a habit, to start an exercise program—that you have not followed through on or stuck with.

So, why would this decision to deal with unresolved issues and chronic problems be any different?" I asked Nat.

In a moment of rare candor, Nat sheepishly admitted that he could not be sure that this time would be any different. Maybe he was doomed to spend his life locked into a vicious cycle of reliving the same conflict with his father over and over again.

"That's a distinct possibility," I responded, choosing not to reassure or rescue him. "But that decision is up to you."

Incredible as it may seem, sometimes changing a life pattern is a matter of conscious choice.

18

6. *Experimenting with Alternative Strategies*

If understanding a predicament or choosing to behave differently were all one had to do to resolve unfinished business or change dysfunctional patterns, we would all be like Dorothy in *The Wizard of Oz*: we could just click our heels together three times and wish ourselves back to Kansas.

Unfortunately, Witches of the East do not leave us alone just because we *understand* they are in a bad mood because a house fell on them. Similarly, deciding to put the past behind us and get on with things is not only a matter of making up our minds to do so. Definite action is required, strategies that are quite different from what you are already doing.

Nat stopped reacting to others as if they were his father. Even more exciting for him, he was finally able to confront his father (rather than surrogates) with his feelings about their relationship. He was able to work through the anger and resentment, even forgive his father to a point where he was able to resume a guarded relationship. Nat no longer allowed himself to be set off by actions that had little to do with the reality of what transpired. That is not to say that he gave up his combative style; actually, he sort of enjoyed a "healthy" fight now and then, especially when it resulted in eventual reconciliation and mutual understanding. However, Nat's fierceness, his frightening power to intimidate, became muted as he exercised increasing control over what he permitted himself to react to and how he chose to respond.

In Chapter One we will approach the subject of what sets *you* off. Who are the people who push your buttons? And what is going on *in you* that makes you so vulnerable to manipulation or hurt?

CHAPTER ONE

Identifying
What Sets You Off

You are reading this book for a very good reason: there is at least one relationship in your life right now, whether with a boss, co-worker, friend, neighbor, sibling, child, parent, or spouse, that is not going the way you would like. You feel at a loss as to how to change long-standing patterns in your relationships. Furthermore, it feels to you as though the conflicts that have developed are not really your fault; it is the other person who is being (choose one) unreasonable/unfair/unrealistic/stubborn/manipulative/cantankerous/uncooperative.

It is certainly true that a number of the people with whom you have had struggles either have chips on their shoulders or have particular personality traits or interpersonal styles that make them difficult for most anyone to get along with. There are certain kinds of people and particular situations that have consistently pushed your buttons. In order to move beyond blame you will have to discover the patterns of your conflicts: Who gets to you? In which situations? Under what circumstances?

The main point of this book is that it does very little good to blame even very difficult people for creating misery or dissatisfaction in your life. Crying "It's you, not me!" may provide temporary relief in that you can sidestep responsibility for the conflict taking place, but it has the distinct side effect of implying that since others are at fault, your only recourse is to wait for them to get their acts together.

Understanding People Who Appear Obstructive

Think about the one relationship in your life right now that is most difficult. Instead of attending to the ways this other person is being manipulative or obstructive or controlling, the ways he or she is unfair or unreasonable, ask yourself who your antagonist reminds you of. It is highly likely that you have encountered someone like him or her before. And just as in the past, with very little effort you can easily recapture feelings of being overwhelmed.

If you conjure an image of the person who is currently your greatest nemesis, you probably can access immediately rage, frustration, resentment, or indignation. "What an unreasonable jerk!" or "What a heartless bitch!" may be your automatic response to even thinking about this person who pushes your buttons. Try to picture the person's face. Hear that voice that grates on your nerves. Feel the intensity of the reactions that immediately bubble to the surface.

Now, for just a minute or two, put these feelings on a shelf. Recall some specific instances in which you have seen this person interact in quite a different manner with other people. So what is it about *you* that invites such dysfunctional interactions with this person, and with this type of person? Why are you especially vulnerable while others remain relatively immune?

While you are reflecting on these queries, consider that there are indeed some people who not only get on your nerves but irritate many others as well. Getting beyond blame means much more than just looking at your own contributions to problems and the circular dynamics of interactive struggles. It also involves educating yourself about people who seem uncooperative or who in some cases are difficult for anyone to deal with because of a consistently dysfunctional interpersonal style.

While some of these people are difficult for anyone to interact with, others are ornery only with you, or only in certain circumstances in which you are involved. This is a crucial distinction: before you can hope to break through obstructive cycles you must be able to distinguish your role in the struggle. In fact, in most instances in which people act uncooperatively, their behavior is inadvertently triggered by the behavior of others—pushing their buttons, playing games with them, trying to control them, withdrawing, being punitive, or aggravating them by being rigid and uncompromising. Nevertheless, difficult people do exist, and otherwise very nice individuals become uncooperative under certain circumstances.

Who Bugs You and Why?

Who gets under your skin with the greatest of ease? Who can provoke you with the least effort? With what kinds of people have you most often struggled and found yourself in conflict? What are some of the ways in which people have treated you that have aggravated you the most?

Don't just *read* these questions, *answer* them! If you have trouble figuring out who most consistently bugs you and who has gotten to you in the past, ask someone who is close to you. If you cannot clarify your thoughts, write them down until a prevalent theme emerges. Don't just skip to the next paragraph without completing this task: the words that follow will only speak directly to you, to your predicament, when you have made the effort to personalize the material.

You have no doubt noticed that there is indeed a pattern to the people who bug you the most. They get to you where you are most vulnerable, if not in your search for universal approval, then in other ways, such as those in the disclosures listed below:

- "I hate to feel unappreciated. I put myself out for people, really extend myself, and then they act like it is their entitlement. I may not say anything at the time, but later I will explode."
- "When people are condescending toward me I work extra hard to try and put them in their place. I'm sure they have no idea what game I am playing. Actually, it isn't a game at all; it is serious business. I will do anything to show them that they can't keep up with me."
- "Whiners. When somebody starts to whine, or even sounds like they are complaining about something, it reminds me of scratching my fingernails along a chalkboard: it makes me grit my teeth. There is no way that I will give in to or negotiate with someone who whines."
- "I don't think very clearly when people try to mother me. I know they are only trying to be helpful, but I become unreasonable and ungrateful. I guess I am trying to discourage them from mothering me, but because I am not very direct in expressing what is going on for me, I only end up hurting their feelings."
- "When people try to take a one-down position I want to

slap them. I just hate the idea of anyone being dependent on or beholden to me. I will start a fight just to get them to stop clinging or demanding anything from me."

- "I have some problems with control issues. I cannot stomach the idea of *anyone* having power over me. I become very stubborn, very reluctant to compromise my freedom in any way."

- "I have a hard time when someone of the opposite sex tries to get close to me. I feel very threatened by that. I am unwilling to risk getting hurt, so I try to chase her away."

- "When somebody appears the slightest bit manipulative, I immediately write him off. I make a decision never to trust him no matter how he might try to redeem himself. I never forget and I never forgive."

- "I have put up with enough abuse in my life. I will not tolerate people raising their voices or even getting in my face. I admit that I tend to overreact a bit, but hey, nobody will *ever* intimidate me again."

- "I set myself up with the same kinds of people over and over again. First, I idealize someone as a mentor. I put him or her on a pedestal, expecting things that no one could possibly deliver, and then feel betrayed because I get disappointed."

This, of course, is but a sampling of the possibilities. Perhaps you recognized yourself in one of these testimonials. If not, you can specify what your own area of personal vulnerability is, where you tend to react in anger disproportionate to the situation. Generally, these patterns tend to fall into several broad groups.

A Typology of Triggers

Whether a conflict involves manipulative/abusive participants or people who are reasonably highly functioning, it almost always is triggered by experiences from the past. We respond to people based not only on what they are doing now but on who they remind us of, how the situations resemble others we have lived through previously, and how we perceive their behavior as filtered through our subjective impressions.

Our perceptions and attitudes are shaped, to a great extent, by our biases, distortions of reality, and sometimes inaccurate interpretations of what others are doing and what their behavior means. That is why it is important to monitor not only what you find disturbing in others but also how you are choosing to interpret their behavior.

From the examples presented in the preceding section of who some people find most provocative, several broad categories emerge. These are the types of situations or people that elicit extreme reactions, such that you feel yourself losing control, your power draining away. These "triggers" fall into several broad groups:

1. Those from Whom You Repeatedly but Unsuccessfully Attempt to Win Approval

There are a few people in your life whose opinions are especially important to you. They may include parents, an older sibling, a supervisor, a mentor or a friend. When these individuals withhold their affirmations, you work even harder to earn their accolades, all the while resenting the extent to which you care what they think.

As one man explains, when such an individual doesn't

respond to you in the way that you would have preferred, conflict is easily triggered:

"My older brother has no idea why I get so mad at him. I call him on the phone and tell him about the new car I bought, the new deal I put together, the great idea I have, and he usually says that it sounds just fine. Then he changes the subject. I realize that I am hanging on every word he says. I wait, holding my breath, for him to tell me I am doing great. When he doesn't give me what I want, I get frustrated and try to impress him even more. He doesn't know what is going on when I yell at him for being so selfish.

"It has been pointed out to me that I am not so much angry at him as I am angry at myself for being so addicted to his approval. That may be so, but the fact remains that he is the one person with whom I find myself most in conflict."

2. Those Who Challenge Your Competence

No matter how much self-assurance we broadcast to the world, deep down inside all of us are insecure. We wonder about what people think of us, and we care deeply that they view us as competent. Yet there are a few people who, either by virtue of their assigned positions in supervisory roles or because they feel it is their duty, let you know that you do not quite measure up to their standards. This could be because what they expect is unreasonable, or it might reflect an accurate assessment of some weakness in need of upgrading. The problem is not so much the fact that someone is pointing out something that you could improve as it is feeling as though your very competence as a human being is being called into question.

"Okay, so I sometimes make mistakes. I don't claim to be

27

perfect. There is this one lady at work who is constantly looking over my shoulder. If I sensed that she was doing so to help
me, perhaps I would not feel so defensive. But she reminds me
of this teacher I had in elementary school who used to delight
in humiliating me every time I made a mistake pronouncing
certain words. My speech problem continued to get worse until I escaped from her clutches.

"Now here is this woman standing over me all of the time,
just waiting for me to screw up so she can point it out to everyone else. I can't abide this type of meddling!"

What is interesting about this particular case is that there
was considerable distorting taking place in this woman's perceptions. After hearing the "meddler's" version of the same
events, it became clear that she *was* attempting to be helpful
but that her actions were constantly being misinterpreted.
Conflicts were continually being ignited, not only by what
was taking place in the present but by traumatic events of the
past.

3. Those with Whom You Fear Intimacy

There are two drives operating simultaneously inside most of
us. One is the intense desire to be close to others, to find and
sustain love, to feel understood and connected. Unfortunately,
this involves considerable vulnerability and risk taking. Hence,
the second drive is self-protection.

The people with whom you would like to feel most intimate
are also those who have the most leverage with which to hurt
you. Because you have more invested in intimate relationships
than you do in acquaintanceships, there is a much greater likelihood of intense conflict. By keeping people at a distance, by

restraining your feelings toward them, you reduce the possibility of being rejected. Conflict is thus one method two or more people use to keep from getting too close.

I have seen this process operate time and again with some single people who claim they are looking for life partners but repeatedly sabotage prospects by manufacturing conflicts in the relationships. As one couple explains, the same scenario is not uncommon between spouses who are half in and half out of their marriages. During separate interviews, I heard the following stories:

> WIFE: Look, he hurt me before. I just can't trust him; he'll do the same thing again. I don't really want to get a divorce. I have heard from friends that being single is no picnic either. But I don't really want to be that close to him. He sometimes brings me flowers, or makes dinner, or tries to be nice, but then I just pick a fight with him. It's a lot safer.

> HUSBAND: I don't know what she told you, but it is certainly not all my fault. She pushes me away. I know there was a time when she wanted to be close to me and I didn't respond, but that is all in the past. Now that I am ready, she claims she no longer cares.

What would happen if the wife broke down her defensiveness and started to respond to her husband's efforts to reach out? They have worked out their little dance so that they take turns being the pursuer and the pursued. That way they never have to risk real intimacy, with its accompanying vulnerability.

4. Those Whom You Experience as Withholding

You may be most consistently stymied by someone who *appears* to prevent you from getting what you want. This person may be *perceived* as controlling or manipulative or even abusive. The choice of the words *appears* and *perceived* is deliberate: they imply that somebody may be difficult to deal with not just because of what he does but because of how you interpret his actions. Every person you fight with has many other people in his life with whom he gets along quite well. *You cannot look at a person who seems difficult to you without also looking at yourself.*

This phenomenon is illustrated in the case of one department in an organization in which the supervisor is perceived as the most difficult person imaginable: "He is totally unfair and arbitrary in his decisions. He is argumentative, even abusive in the ways in which he relates to others. I can't stand being around the guy. All we ever do is disagree."

The plight of this man is substantiated by several of his colleagues, who share his perception of the predicament. He receives support and encouragement from these folks that his assessment of who is at fault for their conflicts is indeed accurate. Yet there is another constituency within this department that finds the supervisor to be quite even handed and reasonable in the decisions that he makes and in the ways in which he relates to others. So what makes their experiences so different? Why do some people encounter such tremendous difficulty in their interactions with this supervisor while others have few problems?

The answer, of course, is that conflict is an *interactive* process. It takes at least two people with different perspectives to have a disagreement. And it usually involves relating to an adversary not only as he objectively appears to you but also as a representative of people from your past. You cannot fight back against the villains who abused you, but, by gosh, you will take no grief from anyone again! Of course, if you are hypervigilant, always looking for people who are trying to hurt you, you will find evidence everywhere. Your trigger point may be set off by the smallest imagined provocation—unless you begin to understand the basis for these reactions.

Boy, Is This Familiar!

Dale has begun to notice that the relationships in which he has had the most trouble, from childhood to the present, have been those in which a particular kind of person refuses to engage with him in an honest exchange. He perceives such individuals as evasive, dishonest, and therefore untrustworthy.

One such person currently in his life, reminiscent of so many others he has struggled with in the past, is Fred, a good-natured guy who for some reason drives Dale crazy with his tendency to avoid confrontation. Fred will do anything in his power to distract them from dealing with what Dale considers to be the problem at hand.

Dale's attempts to keep Fred on track, dealing with the issues, have been met with increasingly inventive ways of staying in safe areas, as demonstrated in this dialogue between the two friends.

DALE: There is something that I would like to straighten out between us.

FRED: Sure. No problem. Could I ask you something first? I need some help with my car.

DALE: I would be happy to help you. But as I mentioned, I want to resolve something that happened before that is still bothering me.

FRED: Fine by me. What's on your mind? Oh yeah, before I forget, since my car isn't working too well, could you give me a ride later?

DALE: Sure. But I really want to talk about this thing that's bothering me.

FRED: Hey, me too. It's just that until I take care of this problem with my car, I can't really concentrate on anything else. Maybe we could talk about this some other time. Did you see that game last night?

Let's give Fred the benefit of the doubt and assume that he is not always so determined to keep the focus of discussions on superficial levels, ignoring important issues in relationships. He is nervous about this matter that Dale brought up. He is afraid that he will be blamed because he senses that he did something wrong. Rather than resolving this issue, his fear of blame drives him to become obstructive in their communication, which drives Dale crazy.

Understanding Why Some People Act Differently from the Way You Might Expect or Prefer

The question remains as to why people act in certain ways, why they attempt to short circuit progress even when it is to their own detriment. Both Dale and Fred are utterly perplexed as to the motives and behavior of the other. They both feel misunderstood. They feel disappointed that the other person is not complying with their expectations.

A crucial factor in figuring out who sets you off and how to neutralize their effects is understanding why some people act the way they do. In order to move beyond blaming others for your plight you will first have to understand that they may be operating under rules that are different from but just as valid as your own. There are thus several reasons why some people will dig their heels in or appear obstructive, even when it is to their own detriment.

They Don't Understand What You Expect

All of us have certain expectations regarding how others should act and how they should treat us. If you are not explicit about these preferences, and do not communicate them clearly enough so that others know what you want, you are likely to feel disappointed or let down.

This predicament is illustrated in the disclosure of one person whose unstated expectations were the source of conflict with someone:

"I was feeling increasingly angry at a friend I meet for lunch. More often than not, it seemed like I was getting stuck paying more than my fair share of the bill. I held on to that resentment for some time—I know it affected our relationship. Finally I said something to my friend about this, and to my surprise, she stated that she thought I preferred to pay more because I order more to eat."

They Lack the Ability to Do What You Want

It is certainly reasonable to expect people to behave in certain ways. Be sure, however, that they have the knowledge and skills to comply with your requests. A conflict between two room-mates started because of unrealistic demands:

"I got really mad at my roommate because when he used my computer, he never cleaned up the mess he made during his computations. I asked him if he knew what he was doing, and he said he did. Then I learned he really didn't know how to do what I was asking, but he was afraid to tell me. He thought I'd be even more critical of him."

They Have Some Emotional Problem

Some people have emotional or other disturbances that make it difficult for them to function appropriately in certain aspects of life, especially interpersonal dimensions. These people are sufficiently impaired that they are unable to respond sensitively and cooperatively during times of conflict. A father shamefully admits how the pressures in his life get the best of him:

"I really wanted to tell my son how much I loved him, that I was sorry for yelling at him the way I did. But I have been under so much stress that I can't seem to keep my temper under control. I just lash out at people even though I don't mean to. As soon as I open my mouth I know I am about to cross some line, but I feel powerless to stop."

They Are Skilled at Using Manipulation to Get Their Way

One reason to be obstructive is that you can make sure that others don't get what they want—even if you lose, too. Manipulation is also helpful in undermining an adversary, recruiting support for one's position, and operating without risk of direct attack. In short, people act this way because it works, as is evident in the following example:

"Look, it's not so much that I don't like the way you're handling things [read: *I don't like the way you are handling things*]; I simply disagree with the policy that has been established. I have been your greatest advocate [*to your face; behind your back, I undermine you every chance I get*]. I really want you to be successful [*only to the extent that it makes me look good*]. You have to trust me [*don't trust me*] if you expect me to help. [*Help? I will make sure you fail with every resource at my disposal*]. It pains me so to see you struggling [*pains me that I can not see more*] and I want to run interference for you [*'interfere' is just about right*]. So now, tell me what is going on with you."

They Don't Perceive Any Incentives to Cooperate

There is no reason to be helpful during negotiations if winning is not more attractive than the struggle itself. Some people thrive on conflict—they like the excitement, passion, and sparks flying. They revel in their power as agitators, and they don't much enjoy periods of tranquility.

"I do like the feeling of exhilaration during heated arguments. In some ways, it's kind of fun: two people going at it with both fists flying. Frankly, I feel depressed when it's all over."

They Are Receiving Secondary Benefits as a Result of Their Behavior

In medical parlance it has been observed that often patients will not recover from surgery or illness because they enjoy the attention and comfort they are receiving. People who are obstructive accrue other payoffs for being difficult: (1) they are able to procrastinate and prevent action; (2) they can inflict damage on others and thereby feel powerful; (3) they can avoid responsibility for their plight and blame others for their misery. Most such people are not aware of what they are doing, as the following example illustrates:

"Sometimes I will deliberately ruin a relationship with someone I care about just so I can stay in control. I end things when I am ready. That way I am rarely rejected by others and I protect myself from being hurt."

They Are Acting Out Unresolved Feelings Toward an Authority Figure

Transference reactions do not occur only in psychotherapy. We are constantly responding to others not as who they are but as who they remind us of, particularly when someone is in an authority or power position.

"There is this guy at work who sets me off no matter what he does. I'm sure he has no idea what this is about. I'm not sure I even know, except that he reminds me of this teacher I had in high school—kind of pompous. I snap at him for no reason, then I notice what I'm doing, back off, and ignore him for the rest of the day."

It is possible, of course, that it is not the other person who is being difficult. You may be the one who is being unreasonable, confusing, or unrealistically demanding. It therefore would be interesting to sort out the extent to which your/his/her obstructive behavior is situational or characterological. In other words, is the difficulty unique to this situation or part of a longstanding style of dealing with others?

Merton, for example, is normally an easygoing guy who prefers to avoid confrontation whenever possible. For some reason, however, he is engaged with Samuel in a series of vicious arguments. Merton refuses to back down, will not give in one iota during negotiations, and has resolutely decided to keep fighting no matter what the outcome. Samuel, by contrast, is used to this kind of emotionally charged situation. It is his nature (or perhaps his training) to make life as difficult as possible for as many people as possible. Samuel is acting in character for him: being obstructive is a way of life. Merton, on the other hand, has *chosen* to be obstructive in this one situation to assert his independence and express his autonomy.

The people who push your buttons come in both varieties: (1) those who are being difficult in response to behavior in you that they perceive as difficult, and (2) those who are characterologically difficult, perhaps even prone to being abusive at times. Since relationships with the latter group are likely to be the most emotionally charged, you will find it even more challenging to "unplug" yourself from chronically unsatisfying patterns with them. Just because it may be more frustrating for you to work through conflicts with the chronically difficult does not mean that you will not be able to do so; it will just involve more energy, commitment, and disciplined action on your part in order to not permit yourself to get out of control.

Seeing Yourself in Others

It was Freud who first conceived of human beings as holding a vast reservoir of psychic energy—internal forces of tension, frustration, aggression, and sexuality that must be released or, more often, displaced through less direct channels. Scapegoating and blaming others, projecting unacceptable impulses onto outsiders, can be viewed as ways to deal with hostile feelings that have no comfortable home. That is why one of the first places to look when you are in the process of finding fault with others is at yourself: What aspects of them that you find so distasteful or despicable are also parts of you?

"None!" you might respond indignantly. How dare I suggest such a thing! Well, look again. More often than not, when you become disproportionately upset with someone else's unacceptable behavior, there is something of yourself that you recognize in the exchange, a part of you that you dislike very much. It is, of course, much easier and safer to be critical of someone else than it is to direct blame inward.

In Chapter Two we continue the journey toward discovering the patterns of your conflicted relationships by moving away from a focus on other people to confronting the kinds of interactions that arouse your deepest fears.

Exploring the Origins and Causes of Your Conflicts

EACH CHAPTER IN THIS BOOK represents a connected step in an overall program to help you identify and work through core issues that lie at the heart of conflict with others. After you have become aware of the kinds of situations and individuals that most consistently trigger unpleasant reactions in you, the next logical stage in the process is to come to terms with what has created these problems for you.

What is it about interpersonal conflict in general that is so personally threatening? I believe one thing; you believe another. I try to convince you that I am right, and you attempt to do the same from your point of view. So what is the big deal? How do our emotions, even our personal self-worth, get caught up in the struggle? And why do particular kinds of argumentative interactions get to us more than others?

Conflicts in relationships are among the most stressful experiences you will ever live through because there is so much at stake, some of it real, some of it mostly illusion. Whether the potential loss is a significant forfeiture of your resources or only the perception that you are diminished in status, basically all of the stress comes down to anticipating either a loss of territory (position, power, money) or a loss of face.

To manage the side effects of conflict you must choose different ways of responding to the stress of these critical encounters. This involves recognizing what is really in jeopardy for you: are the risks real or are they distortions based on over-reactions? Naturally, blame plays a major role in this scenario. The more you assign guilt outside of yourself, the more stress levels initially will be reduced; since you are not at fault, you do not have to feel the least bit responsible. Eventually, however, this strategy will come back to haunt you as you consider your own sense of powerlessness—you will come to feel that conflicts are circumstances that are thrust upon you rather than situations in which you are an active participant.

The Conflicts in Your Life

It is important for you to realize how and why certain kinds of conflicts get to you more than others. Once you recognize and can anticipate your vulnerable areas, you can be ready to bolster them with added reinforcements. Say, for example, you notice that your first line of counterattack (in your head or out loud) in conflict situations is to offer a feeble denial—"I didn't do it. It wasn't me."—only to be met with more vigorous, convincing arguments that you did in fact play a role (an easy task since it is true). You can short-circuit this normally ineffective coping style and try something else: "It is beside the point as to who did what. Let's try to figure out what we can do to repair the damage."

Before you can ever solve a problem you first must have an accurate diagnosis. To say that you are involved in a conflicted relationship is about as informative as telling a doctor that you don't feel well. The doctor would want to know where it hurts, when it hurts, what the pain feels like, what you have discovered that seems to lessen the discomfort, and so on. Unfortunately for us, although physicians have magnetic imagery, computer simulations, and other technological wizardry to aid them in identifying problems, we are left to speculate and draw conclusions based on intuition and reasoning. Nevertheless, I suspect you already have some solid clues as to what the characteristic patterns of the conflicts in your life are all about.

If you spend a few hours musing about the troubled relationships you have encountered, they may, at first, seem quite different from one another. One was with a childhood friend who betrayed you. Perhaps another involves chronic tension with a parent or child. A third is with somebody at work. But although the kinds of relationships involved may be different, the patterns of the conflicts may be essentially the same.

Some Questions to Ask Yourself

It makes sense that in the process of discovering the patterns of your conflicts you also will uncover their origins; in some ways, it is impossible to look at one without the other. As you begin to recognize a consistent picture, one in which you consistently fall for the same traps and engage in the same ineffective attempts to rectify matters, you cannot help but muse about how and why this pattern developed.

Go back to your personal collection of significantly conflicted relationships that have occurred throughout your life. Whether you complete this task on paper or address these issues inside your head, you will find it helpful to ask yourself a number of questions in order to help make the patterns more clear.

1. What Were the Initial Triggers for the Relationship Turning Sour?

Think back to what sparked your most significant current conflict. It was probably not so much a single incident as it was a series of misunderstandings over time, eventually culminating in an explosion of outrage, frustration, or indignation. If you attempt to recreate the sequence of events you may find a scenario unfolding similar to the following described by a mother who is estranged from one of her daughters. The mother was especially vulnerable to that type of situation mentioned in the previous chapter in which someone she loved withheld affection and approval.

"I suppose our troubles first began after the divorce; she had a lot of resentment toward me for leaving her father. Perhaps she had harbored some strong negative feelings even before then, but I am most aware that the conflict between us started to intensify at about the time we relocated to a new area. It was as if she hated me for disrupting her life that had been going so smoothly at the time.

"There had always been a degree of competition between us—not so much an oedipal thing, competing for her father's attention, as an insecurity on my part that maybe I wasn't a good enough mother. My own mother was so negligent when I was a child that I vowed to be different. I think my daughter sensed this vulnerability in me, and at times she would exploit it to get what she wanted. I don't mean to imply that this freeze between us is all her fault; quite the contrary, I know that because I tried so hard to be the perfect mother for her I didn't draw the line when I should have.

"Anyway, we patched things up for a while after the divorce, got along all right except for the normal squabbles that parents and children have. Then I started to worry about her, maybe even feeling guilty for doing what I wanted at the expense of my children. I started to give in to her more when I know I should have stood my ground. That is exactly what I had done before—with my ex-husband, with one of my sisters, certainly with my boss. I give in to them hoping that they will then back off and let me be. But now I realize that I just end up appearing weak and spineless.

"The pattern that has emerged for me is that in my effort to avoid confrontation, I give in to people. I so badly want to be liked that I don't stand up for myself; that has been especially true with my daughter. Now she respects me so little that we hardly ever talk at all. When we do speak, I can hear her voice dripping with sarcasm. I then become even more contrite and apologetic. Before we know it, we both can't wait to hang up.

"I now realize that the origin of most of my conflicts is lodged in this need I have for others' validation and approval. Until I am willing to face up to the responsibility that comes with being in a relationship, including telling others what I want, I know that I will continue to have problems."

Before this woman can expect to change the patterns of conflicted relationships in her life, she needs to not only identify what sets her off but figure out the origins and causes of these dysfunctional interactions. By recognizing how the pattern of conflict with her daughter paralleled that of other disagreements she had experienced during her life—all in an effort to gain the approval and validation she could never get from her own mother—she was able to loosen the hold of this habitual behavior.

Likewise, before you can change an enduring pattern in your life, you must have some understanding as to how and why things developed the way they did. This is especially true with regard to why you experience such strong emotional reactions to certain people and situations and not to others.

2. What Are Your Strongest Emotional Reactions and Fears Sparked by These Conflicts?

What is at stake for you that feels so threatening, so anxiety provoking, that you can hardly think straight, much less respond in a calm, deliberate manner?

As you increase your awareness of your characteristic reactions during conflicts, as well as what kinds of disputes trigger which emotional responses in you, you increase the likelihood that you can do something different from what you normally would do in those situations. An internal dialogue along these lines might go something like this:

Wait a minute. What's going on? Why am I feeling so threatened right now? What reason might I have to be so defensive? What do I believe is at stake that makes me willing to become so heated over a seemingly inconsequential matter? How is this situation similar to others that I have experienced? What do I normally do in such predicaments that I want to avoid doing this time?

The answers to these questions can be found in the personal conceptions you have formulated as to what you are really arguing about. It is not just a matter of which of us will make a decision this time, or who will get his or her way, or whether we will eat in this restaurant or that one; there are much larger issues at stake, concerns that reach into the heart of your very being and threaten your sense of self-worth. As one man I interviewed explained:

"To most of the people who know me I seem very secure. I have cultivated this image carefully. It's not really an image. I mean, I *am* secure most of the time. But underneath my calm exterior there is a very fragile child. I take criticism very personally. The strongest message I learned from my father growing up was to never let people get the best of me. The times I can recall when I disappointed my father in school or sports, he made it very clear that what I had done previously meant absolutely nothing. Forget that I scored two touchdowns in the last game; what had I done in *this* game?

"As much as I have accomplished in my career, with friends, with my wife and children, I still hear my father's voice, which now sounds suspiciously like my own asking myself what I have done lately. Maybe I don't have it anymore. Maybe I lost my power.

"What this means is that after all these years I am still trying to prove myself. I can't seem to let go. I'm still on probation in my own mind. When someone questions something that I said or did, I just have to take that person on. I know this means that I find myself in quite a number of arguments, but I don't feel I have much choice. If I don't defend myself I will look bad to others, and also to me."

This fear of losing face is what nudges him to stay in conflict far longer than he needs or wishes to. He has told himself that he cannot afford to shoulder any blame whatsoever because then others might think less of him. At the very least, he will feel diminished in his own eyes. Now imagine the kind of stress this man puts himself through during the most pedestrian of disagreements—who bought lunch last time or who was primarily responsible for that lost account. Think about what it would be like for you to try to settle an argument with this fellow. There is no way that he will ever give in. That is but one reason why conflicts arise, escalate, and continue on toward destructive proportions.

The key to diminishing the control that your deepest fears and threats to your internal security have over you involves, first of all, understanding exactly which fears in you are being massaged by others. Two of the most common are the need for control and the need for acceptance.

The need for control. Each of us was born out of control, completely at the mercy of others to feed us, keep us warm and dry, protect us, and keep us safe. As we grew older and more self-sufficient, we struggled with our parents, teachers, and other adults for the right to make our own decisions and control our own destiny. There was usually some disagreement between our own perceptions of what we were capable of doing and what others, who held the power, believed we ought to be doing.

Now you are an adult, perfectly capable of making decisions concerning any aspect of your life. Yet there are other people—family and friends—who have strong preferences regarding what they believe you should be doing. Also wanting to control you are people who have some authority (legitimate or self-imposed) to influence and guide you in particular directions that they feel are most appropriate.

The struggle for your independence, freedom, and autonomy is thus a major force in your life. Anyone who is in a position to restrict your movements, any situation in which you feel less freedom than you would prefer, is likely to elicit your fear of losing control.

This is the single most powerful fear that I struggle with on a daily basis. It not only sparks my most intense emotional reactions during interpersonal encounters, but it also lurks just beneath the surface during most of my waking moments. Thus when somebody else attempts to tell me what to do, to exercise some authority over me, to control me in any way, I react most vehemently to resist their efforts. This rebelliousness can easily be traced to my earliest years, and it has abated minimally during the decades since then. But it is surprising, even to me, to realize the extent to which my need for control or, more accurately, my fear of losing control, operates in my daily life.

When I stand on a balcony, or the side of a cliff, I sometimes feel an irresistible urge to jump off—not because I want to die; on the contrary, I love life so much that I try to squeeze out of it every moment of satisfaction that I possibly can—but because I wonder what it would be like to lose control, just for a moment, and go flying off the edge. That's all it would take, a single instant of decision, and I would be sailing into oblivion. I have similar thoughts during many other daily encounters in which I flirt with the idea that the control I work so hard to maintain is a very tenuous condition indeed.

Knowing this about myself helps me maintain a degree of vigilance over how my control issues are triggered by the actions of others. Having felt very little control as a child, I am unwilling to surrender any part of the autonomy that I have worked so hard to achieve. I could not stop my parents from divorcing. I could not join the most popular groups in school. I could not stop my body from expressing its needs in ways that left me feeling more like a passenger than the one in charge. I could not have the kinds of relationships that I wanted with people growing up. Most of the time, I did not feel like I had the slightest control over what I was feeling. But as an adult in the prime of life, nobody will tell me what to do ever again.

Do you think this propensity of mine to maintain control in my life has something to do with overreacting to situations in which conflict results?

The need for acceptance. Beneath the veneer of self-assurance and the image of competence we present to the world, most of us feel unworthy of others' respect and affection. You may appear quite confident, handling situations as if you know exactly what you are doing and where you are headed, but there are always nagging doubts whispering in your ear:

"You don't really know what you are doing. You are just pretending."

"People don't really like and respect you as much as you think they do. You are just blind to their true feelings about you."

"What you have accomplished in life is not all that important. You are deluding yourself if you think that anything you do really makes a difference in the big scheme of things."

You may act as if what people think about you really does not matter, that your own opinion is all that counts. You may pretend to be oblivious to others' disapproval, as long as you know that you are right. You may tell yourself that being accepted by others is nice but not really necessary. The truth of the matter is that you desperately want to be accepted and valued by others. Losing the support of the people you are closest to would leave you floating through life completely on your own, with nobody you could count on but yourself. This might satisfy your need for control, but it would foster feelings of alienation and isolation.

Some of your most intense emotional reactions and deepest fears are therefore lodged in your strong desire to be accepted by others. You will sometimes compromise your most sacred beliefs, back down from a dispute, or initiate a conflict with someone, all in the name of maintaining your stature in other people's eyes as well as your own self-image. This definitely proved to be the case with Susan, a woman in her forties who found herself involved in a number of disagreements but unable to figure out what they were really about.

An accomplished business woman, Susan often finds herself embroiled in disputes both with her colleagues and with her friends. These conflicts drain a lot of her physical, emotional, and creative energy. She claims that she hates arguing with others, yet she can think of three different relationships in her life in which that is all they do. After an encounter with any one of these people, Susan feels depleted, frustrated, abused, and angry.

For a long time Susan blamed others for treating her with insufficient respect and regard. She held strongly to the belief that she was getting a rotten deal from others who did not appreciate her.

But recently she had begun to recognize a pattern: certain themes had been playing themselves out since she was very young. As a child, she had worked very hard to be the perfect little girl. Her parents doted on her, as long as she was compliant and did what they said. She was comfortable in the role of teacher's pet at school, which meant that she worked very hard to figure out what adults wanted from her and then delivered what was expected without a whimper of protest.

Throughout her life, Susan had looked toward external sources to validate her worth as a human being. As long as she was getting "A's" in school and was the favorite of her parents, teachers, and supervisors, as long as she was the most popular or competent person in a group, she felt just fine about herself. But whenever this image of perfection was jeopardized and she sensed the slightest disappointment or disapproval from others, the only way she could live with herself was to convince those around her that she really was the absolute best. Of course, she was not so much convincing them as she was reassuring herself. The effect, however, was the same: whenever Susan felt that she was not thoroughly and completely accepted by the people whose opinions mattered the most (especially a particular colleague and the two friends with whom she was most often in conflict), she would push things to the point where they would become quite heated.

"So, what you are saying is that you think I don't know what I am doing? I'll have you know . . . Oh, you didn't mean that? Well, then what *did* you mean? You do have this tendency, after all, to start fights when you don't get your way. . . . What do you mean *I* am the one who is always starting the arguments? I would never . . . "

Susan and her associate at work are now engaged in a familiar struggle, one that has repeated throughout her life whenever somebody did not endorse completely what she was doing and communicate that she was being "the perfect little girl," the "teacher's pet," the consummate professional. What is at stake for Susan is the fear that unless she counteracts every perceived criticism, she will be written off by others as unworthy as a friend or colleague. She has kept herself on probation her whole life, feeling that she is only as good as the wonderful things she has done lately. So what if she put four successful deals together without a glitch, or that she has been consistently responsive in a friendship for years? It is her misguided belief that if she messes up just one time, everything goes down the tubes. That is why certain relationships evoked such strong, threatening feelings in her, why she was prone to externalize the blame and direct responsibility elsewhere if at all possible. Creating conflict became a way for her to convince others to back down and not attack her credibility or her delusions of perfection. She would inadvertently—if not deliberately—find herself escalating minor disagreements into full-fledged conflicts because of her fear of compromising her image of perfection.

3. What Expectations Do You Hold That May Be Escalating the Conflict?

The next logical area to explore, after you have begun to identify the patterns of your disputes and their origins and causes, is to consider as honestly as possible what specific things you are doing to make matters worse. Much of the problem, you will find, is centered in the often unrealistic and unreasonable expectations you hold for others.

When you hold certain assumptions that seem quite reasonable to you but that others are not willing or able to abide by, you are likely to feel disappointed and find yourself in conflict situations. Some of the expectations that are most likely to land you in trouble or escalate conflicts are those in which you make demands of other people based on the standards you apply to yourself:

I am willing to go this far and give this much, so he should do the same.

Unless she recognizes how hard I have worked on this, then there is no sense in my continuing.

51

Why doesn't he see that I am not trying to hurt him? I am just trying to help.

I did my part; now it is her turn to do just as much.

The problem with expectations such as these is that: (1) other people cannot read our minds and know what we expect, (2) just because we live by certain rules does not mean that others must do so as well, and (3) such expectations set things up so that blame can be placed elsewhere when things do not work out.

Ironically, this last cause of conflict is both the most painful and the one you are in the most powerful position to do something about. This category of conflict is essentially self-inflicted: by holding certain expectations of others, and making demands that they are unwilling to meet (because they have a different set of expectations for *you* that *you* are not meeting), disputes over responsibility and fault are highly likely.

The logical antidote for resolving these kinds of disputes involves checking out your expectations for others, holding them up to the clear light of day to assess their appropriateness, and then making them explicit. When the other person is willing to articulate just as clearly what it is that he or she expects from you, then you are well on your way to negotiating some common ground.

This means that when you become aware that there is tension between yourself and someone else, an alternative choice to blaming that person for being unreasonable is to check out what it is that you are expecting that he or she may not be willing or able to do. This is highlighted in the following example of a couple who had been married for fifteen years but who had continued to fight with one another over seemingly inconsequential matters. Both Joan and Jason shared their different expectations for one another and for the marriage.

JASON: A marriage is a partnership in which two people have made a commitment to one another to work toward common goals. I don't mean to include just large-scale goals such as raising a family or putting away a retirement fund, but also doing things together. I know Joan thinks that I smother her, that I demand too much of her. But she is my best friend. I just want to be with her as much as possible, to share our lives together. As my wife, she should want to spend as much time as possible with me, to be available so that we can do things together. If only she would spend more time at home I think we could get along much better.

Jason expects marriage to be a close relationship in which the partners do as much as possible together. They not only have common interests, but they also make an effort to accommodate the other rather than going off on their own. Jason believes that if only Joan would be more attentive, more available to meet his needs, more accommodating to what he expects of her, then they would not have any disagreements. This perspective is quite different from Joan's ideas.

JOAN: I feel smothered by him. He wants me at his beck and call. I love the man, I really do. But I will not live my life for him; I have my own interests, some of which are quite different from his. I don't think a marriage can or should meet all of one's needs. If only Jason would back off and not push me so much, if only he would give me some space and time to pursue my own interests, then I wouldn't have to bicker with him so much.

Jason and Joan have differing expectations for their marriage and their mates. When each of them was helped to discover the origins of these ideas about what a good marriage should be, both were able to see how and why their different assumptions were exacerbating their mutual feelings of resentment. Joan came from a home in which she had watched helplessly as her mother had been beaten down and humiliated by her father. Although their relationship did not follow a parallel pattern, Joan had resolved long ago that she would never give away her power the way her mother had. By contrast, Jason defined his notions of marriage based on what he had grown up with. His parents had modeled a very close, perhaps even enmeshed relationship. They did everything together and spent every waking moment in each other's company. It was not unusual, therefore, that Jason would expect that he and Joan would negotiate similar roles.

The problem was that Jason and Joan had no intention or inclination to satisfy each other's expectations. Conflict between them was inevitable, at least until they stopped asking for things that were not going to be responded to in the ways they expected. When the texture of their interactions changed to an emphasis on finding out what the other partner was willing to do rather than making demands, they found considerable room for negotiation. Jason realized that he was, in fact, open to renegotiating a different relationship from the one they had originally created fifteen years earlier. Joan, in turn, felt much more inclined to spend quality time with her husband when it felt like it was her choice to do so rather than giving in to emotional blackmail.

Stay with the Real Issue

The object in figuring out the real issues that underlie your *apparent* disagreements is so that you may more accurately target your efforts toward dealing with what is really bothersome rather than with elements that are superficial, distracting, or otherwise irrelevant to the important issues at hand. We have discussed, for example, how your conflicts may represent your attempts to relive dysfunctional patterns that were programmed in the past—when you learned to be dependent on others, to keep people at a distance, or to avoid being hurt. There also may be behaviors that were part of growing up in your family and that you still use in relating to others—playing a subservient role, being a go-between for others in conflict, or having to fight furiously for attention, approval, or control.

It should be apparent by now that most of the things you fight about are not what you are really concerned with; there are other issues, some readily apparent and some buried from view, that drive your behavior. There is no way that you can ever truly resolve disputes until you know what it is that you are actually fighting and feeling upset about.

For example, two friends appear to be having an argument about who will pick up whom to attend a function together. Their underlying issues are noted in italics.

SARA: I guess I could drive. *I don't want to drive. I always drive.*
TINA: Fine. If you don't mind. *What is her problem? She acts like she is doing me a favor.*

SARA: No big deal. I will have to . . . oh, never mind. I'll pick you up. *I don't have any gas. She never offers gas money, either.*

TINA: No maybe I should drive this time. You drove last time. *She probably keeps score.*

SARA: *True. I did drive last time. I drive every time. But if I let her drive, she will get on my case about something else.* Hey, I *said* I would drive. Just tell me what time to pick you up.

TINA: *No way am I going to be indebted to her for this. She'll make me pay.* I think I'll go by myself since I have to do some errands along the way.

SARA: Fine. Maybe I'll see you there. *Not if I can help it.*

As in so many conflicts, these friends are not talking about what the real issues are. They have no idea about the origins and causes of their intense emotional reactions. They appear to be negotiating about who will drive to the function, but each person is really harboring resentments about perceived inequities from the past. If they were able to stop the exchange long enough to ask themselves, "What are we really fighting about?," there is a greater likelihood that they would be able to identify and address their underlying issues and find a mutual solution.

A Summary of Major Themes

There is more to a conflict than just the interactional issues between people: you are also carrying around your own deep-seated issues. To find out what you are fighting about with another person you must be sure of which of your own issues are at stake. The focus of this chapter has been to help you recognize variations of the following themes:

Problems of authority. People who have been in positions of power over you (parents, teachers, bosses) may have exploited or abused you in the past. As a result, you now tend to overreact to anyone you perceive to be in a controlling role.

Problems of personal freedom. You may have an unusually great need for autonomy and independence. You will oppose any effort to restrict your freedom of movement or limit your choices.

Problems of intimacy. You have suffered deep wounds earlier in life that now predispose you to overprotect yourself against hurt or rejection. You are unwilling to allow yourself to get close to people and so use conflict as a way to maintain a safe distance.

Problems of enmeshment. You allow yourself to become overly entangled, perhaps even dependent, on a few people you are close to. You feel both grateful for them and resentful that you are so needy.

Problems of the need for approval. Throughout your life you have been searching for validation, a state that is always short-lived. Since you hang in the balance of how others judge you, conflicts result when you feel disappointed by their assessments.

Of course, this is hardly an exhaustive list of the possibilities; rather, it is a mere sampling of the themes you may have discovered are operative for you. These are the problems you will need to monitor most closely during times of greatest stress, for nothing will escalate a conflict faster than plugging in to your old unresolved issues.

Keep in mind that some degree of discomfort is not altogether a bad thing. In the next stage of the process, described in Chapter Three, you will learn how pain can be harnessed as a force that motivates you to take constructive action.

Allowing Yourself the Discomfort

WHAT PLACE, you may justifiably be wondering, does encouraging pain have in a program to help people who are already struggling with conflict? Am I encouraging self-inflicted suffering as a distraction from wounds inflicted by others? Am I advocating some perverse form of self-torture? Can't you just skip this step and go on to the next chapters, where you get to initiate some fun changes in your life?

Unfortunately, no.

When Discomfort Becomes Your Friend

One of the most difficult concepts for beginning therapists to comprehend is the idea that in order for people to make needed changes in their lives they often must be helped to feel perfectly miserable about themselves the way they presently are. A beginning helper's first instinct when someone cries is to offer him or her a tissue. When a person is obviously struggling with something difficult, the tendency is to pave the way to make it easier. There is no crime in offering comfort, but if the goal is to change a long-standing pattern, discomfort is potentially the greatest of allies rather than an enemy.

Rarely does anyone initiate changes unless what they are already doing is not working very well. People do not walk away from marriages that are perfectly satisfying or even marginally not meeting their needs; they usually feel quite desperate and unhappy by the time they take action, and even then they do so very reluctantly. People do not quit their jobs and make other dramatic life changes unless they are extremely dissatisfied with the way things have been going. A certain amount of tears, anguish, reluctance, depression, anxiety, and misery is par for the course. These come with the territory of altering life patterns that, however self-destructive, are nevertheless familiar.

One of the principal jobs of a therapist, or of any change agent, is not only to help the client feel good about him or herself but also to help him or her feel lousy about some of the ways in which he or she has been managing life. I become concerned and suspicious not when a client complains that she feels terrible about herself when she engages in interactive patterns that have gotten her into trouble, but rather when she reports that she is feeling better about herself even though she is doing the same old things. It takes a certain degree of pain to motivate action.

When Pain Motivates Action

Just a few years ago, I had myself convinced that I was quite satisfied with the way my life had been going. Yes, I was a little bored with the routine of a job that had become predictable, unchallenging, and stressful. I told myself, however, that at least I was earning a good income and that I did seem to be helping people. Whenever I started to feel some discomfort stemming from the whispers inside my head asking me if perhaps there was not something more to life, I quickly shut that voice down. I bribed it by treating myself with a gift. I ignored it by pretending that it was normal to feel dissatisfied with what one is doing. I buried myself in relationships with my family and friends, hoping that eventually the voice (and discomfort) would give up and go away. I tried to convince myself that the conflicts I was experiencing with some of the people in my life were perfectly acceptable.

What a hypocrite I was! Day after day I was telling my clients to take risks, to go after what they wanted in life, to not settle for mediocrity. I urged them to go after their dreams and I supported them along the way. Even worse, I pretended to be a perfect model of all that they should strive to be. Indeed, several clients told me repeatedly how much they admired the way I conducted my life.

No matter how much I tried to deny it, my discomfort grew. During consultations with colleagues, conversations with friends and family, dialogues with myself inside my head and in my journal, I started to become more aware of the issues that were involved. I was able to identify some of the patterns that I was repeating, as well as come to terms with the origins of certain themes. Yet rather than feeling better about myself and where I was headed, I started to feel much worse. Mild depression became my constant companion. I appeared distracted and irritable. Within a five-month period I had four automobile accidents, even though I had gone fifteen years without a single previous incident. Clearly, I was feeling more and more discomfort with myself and the life that I was leading. I had to do something, *anything* other than what I was already doing. No matter how frightened I was of initiating some changes, I realized that nothing could be worse than what I was already experiencing.

A friend and fellow therapist remarked to me one day that I finally looked to her the way she had sensed I had been feeling all along. When was I going to realize that until I made some needed changes my pain would be my lifelong companion? Although I had said that very thing to my clients a thousand times, I could not hear my own voice through the fog of my pain. But my friend's words got through to me, enough so that I finally did take some steps to realign my priorities. This was no easy task. As you might imagine, or recall from your own experiences initiating major life changes, I resisted every step of the way. Couldn't I just go on living the way I was, perhaps make a few minor adjustments, and somehow avoid disrupting things in such an annoying and inconvenient manner?

Hating pain as much as the next person, I did everything within my power to avoid further discomfort. It was like having an excruciating backache: I knew it wouldn't go away without treatment, but I didn't want to do anything radical. Maybe if I just changed my position a bit, the pain would be more tolerable. Perhaps I could simply "medicate" myself with a stronger dose of painkillers, which in my case involved bribing myself with some indulgence (which ultimately only made things worse). Obviously, major "surgery" was needed, even if I was fearful that the cure would be even worse than the problem. Like so many people I have listened to over the years, I preferred a pain that was familiar to one that was unknown—that is, until things became so intolerable that I couldn't go on any longer lying to myself.

This process took several years of hard work. Following the

stages set forth within this book, I eventually came to terms with the realization that my pain was not something to be avoided but something to be embraced as my best friend. Without the tremendous anguish that I felt, the pain that I could no longer ignore, there was no way that I would have ever taken the risky but necessary steps to rewrite the plan of my life.

I give you fair warning that what I am attempting to do is increase, not decrease, your discomfort. I want to get in your face, to confront you with the realization that nothing in your life will change, none of your conflicted relationships will ever be any different, none of your core issues will ever be resolved, unless you let yourself feel your pain to the extent that you can't stand it any longer.

When you turn up the heat enough, you will have no choice but to do some things differently. When you face the fact that certain relationships are not good for you, you will no longer be able to put up with them the way they are. Your only choices will be to: (1) change the pattern of your interactions, (2) think differently about them, or (3) act differently so you no longer subject yourself to misery. But to continue the way things are would be absolutely intolerable and unacceptable!

Helping Yourself Feel More Miserable

If you agree with the premise that we are exploring together— that by allowing yourself to experience your discomfort you will feel greater resolve to change—then your principal task should be to make yourself feel worse, not better. I do not mean that you should subject yourself to suffering just for the sake of practice; the object is to make yourself feel even more miserable when you engage in behaviors that are obviously self-defeating.

63

Joslyn, for example, has become accustomed to a degree of misery in her relationship with her boyfriend, James. They bicker with one another constantly—over how they should spend their time, with whom they should socialize, and where their relationship is going. Joslyn would very much like a permanent relationship, but James is unwilling to commit himself to marriage, now or in the future.

Joslyn and James have been seeing each other long enough for Joslyn to have grown used to the frustrating nature of their relationship. Rarely are her needs met, but then she does not feel entitled to any more than she is getting because of what she observed in her parents' relationship. Joslyn grew up in a home in which her mother and father defined marriage as an endless series of disputes in which Dad always ended up making Mom cry. What Joslyn was living in her own life did not seem unusual to her.

Joslyn relates a story in which James had been watching a football game with his friends. He called her to come over "to keep him company," their code phrase for having sex. Obediently, she drove over to his house and meekly walked past the guys watching the game to follow James into the bedroom. Five minutes after the sex was over, James asked her to go home so he could watch the rest of the game with his friends. Naturally, she acquiesced. The amazing thing about this incident was that Joslyn did not have enough dignity to feel humiliated by this encounter.

If Joslyn was ever to get her needs met in a relationship, if she was ever to move beyond blaming James for their conflicts, if she was ever to feel strong enough to stand up for what she deserved, she had to feel even more miserable about her predicament in order to change it. Rather than offering her only sympathy and support (I had already tried that with little effect), I attempted to increase her level of discomfort in several ways that I would like to suggest to you.

Apply What You Learned About the Causes and Origins of Your Plight

Based on what you now understand about who gets to you most easily and why, what are some ways you can see that you are living in the past rather than in the present? Just because you have reacted to certain people and certain situations in a particular way before does not mean that you have to do so now or in the future. It is lazy and neglectful of you to automatically follow the pattern that was created long ago.

Joslyn became a bit defensive when I confronted her with this challenge. How dare I tell her that the reason she ends up in similar conflicts is because she stubbornly refuses to break the mold she has become comfortable with! "Comfortable! *Comfortable!* You think I like being in this kind of horrid relationship?"

I didn't back down. "Yes, I do think that in many ways you have taught yourself to accept and expect a degree of misery as your birthright. If anyone had treated me the way James treated you, I would have been long gone. But, then, your pain threshold is so high that you are still there asking for more."

This dialogue continued over a period of many hours. The sole object of my confrontation was to help Joslyn feel even more miserable with her predicament. It worked, too. The next time James called her to "keep him company," she did go to his house, but she felt utterly terrible about herself during their interaction. The next time she backed down during a conflict rather than standing up for her rights, she could hardly stand herself. Slowly, inexorably, the anger directed toward James for being so insensitive was coming back toward herself. After all, *she* was the one who was volunteering to put up with the relationship the way it was.

Ask yourself the same questions I asked Joslyn: What are you doing that makes you dislike yourself and that you need to feel even worse about? What do you understand about the patterns of conflict that you are repeating out of fear, neglect, laziness, reluctance to venture out of your comfort zone?

Stare at Your Reflection in the Toilet

This is more of a metaphor than an actual suggestion (although I have, on occasion, asked people to do this). You can probably feel yourself resist the necessary task of allowing yourself to feel the discomfort over continued dysfunction in conflict. That is understandable: very few people want to deal with *more* pain and aggravation, even if it might lead to some long-term gain. To prove my point, I would only have to ask you how many times you have made promises, started diets or exercise programs, that you knew would be good for you in the long run, but in the short term you were unwilling to subject yourself to the deprivation and discomfort involved. Everyone wants to eat healthfully, feel slim and vigorous, follow through on what they commit themselves to, but who has the resolve to put up with the pain?

When I asked Joslyn to "stare into the toilet," what I was asking her to do was to intensify her own self-loathing over being so deferential. Most people have prior associations with staring at their reflection in the porcelain-housed water during times

66

of great sickness. You have had too much to drink or you have the flu. Your head is swimming. You are not sure if you want to vomit, but you are fairly certain that you want to die. You don't think you have ever felt so sick in your life. And then you see your own pitiful reflection staring back at you from inside the toilet. These are the times when you are likely to make some promises to yourself. Never again!, you tell that other self in the water, hoping he or she will think you sincere enough to allow you to vomit and get it over with.

"Okay, okay! I get the point," Joslyn pleaded. "You want me to vomit at the prospect of repeating my same old stupid patterns when James and I start arguing. Well, truthfully, I feel like throwing up every time I think about the fact that I turned out to be just like my mother. I hated her for being so passive, and now look at me!"

Staring at your reflection in the toilet is a reminder of the promises you have made that you have not kept. If you are going to take responsibility for your situation without blaming others, and then to commit yourself to act differently, you will need to draw on the image of how disgusting you find yourself when you are curled on the floor, draped over the lip of the toilet, staring at the rejected contents of your stomach.

Stay with the Pain Rather Than Hiding from It

It is not enough to access your pain, smile proudly as if to say, "See, I found it," and then throw it back whence it came. Once you have realized the degree of your own participation in dysfunctional patterns of conflict, you have to let the wound fester a bit, drain the infection and pus, before you put on the antiseptic to let it heal. I am not suggesting that you take on the role of martyr, suffering in silence. I am only recommending that you not run away from your pain just because it is difficult.

Joslyn stopped seeing me for a while when it became apparent that we had no easy solution for her problem. This went far beyond her relationship with James. She had identified similar kinds of conflicted relationships with her parents, prior lovers, and even people at work. The revelations became so distressing for her that she bolted. I respected her need for time to think through whether she was prepared to live with a different, more intense kind of pain in order to someday free herself of the prison she had chosen for herself. Several months went by before I saw her again. What I saw this time was a renewed resolve in her to stay with her discomfort for as long as it would take to reach her ultimate goal.

It took tremendous courage for Joslyn to stay with her pain as long as necessary to complete the work of self-restoration. We live in a society in which there is little dignity or respect associated with suffering. We are encouraged to "medicate" ourselves whenever possible. You are feeling a little anxious? Have a drink. You are nervous about something? Take a tranquilizer. Feeling depressed? I heard doctors give you pills for that sort of thing. Having problems in your relationship? Get a divorce and start over. Whenever we are confronted with situations that involve tolerating annoyance, inconvenience, discomfort, our very first priority is to find a way to make the pain go away.

As I said earlier in this chapter, there are times when pain can be your most valued ally, signaling to you that everything is not operating as it should. It is a constant reminder that you must take care of your wounds, do some things differently. Assuming that the discomfort is manageable, that it is bringing your attention to something you need to change, stay with it. Don't run away. Don't medicate yourself. There is honor in living with pain, temporarily, when it leads you to some greater good.

Find the Meaning in Your Suffering

The psychiatrist Viktor Frankl, interned in the Nazi concentration camps, once observed that what determined whether people survived their ordeal depended very much on whether they could find some meaning to their suffering. People most often perished when they simply gave up, when they could find no purpose in their torture. Those who were able to create some sense of mission, even if it was just to tell the world about what happened, were much more likely to survive.

Pain can either destroy you or save you, depending on what you do with it. Many people take their own lives when they can find no hope, no way out of their predicament. Similarly, people reconcile themselves to lives of mediocrity, relationships of eternal conflict, and continued dysfunctional patterns when they can see no other choices. Under such circumstances, pain keeps you in line, stops you from trying anything new. It is like having a bad back that sends out excruciating bolts of fire every time you move. Finally, you find a comfortable position that affords some relief. It is unlikely that you will voluntarily move from that position unless you absolutely have to.

Yet when you can find or create some meaning in your suffering, it attains a noble purpose, some underlying reason that makes it worth all the aggravation. I asked this question of Joslyn: "What have you learned from a lifetime of pain?" She spoke more eloquently than I ever could have imagined about her

vision of herself as a kind of Joan of Arc. The difference, however, was that she did not intend to let herself be burned to
death. She was getting herself off the stake to which she had
tethered herself. Meanwhile, she could put up with things a
little longer, knowing that there was a good reason: she had
to buy some more time until she felt strong enough to implement the new plan for her life.

It is easier for you, as well, to put up with the annoyances,
inconveniences, and discomfort of your temporary predicament
if you know that your suffering is worthwhile. This is no different from subjecting yourself to the pain of an exercise regimen,
knowing that you are doing something good for your body.

The challenge, then, is for you to create some purpose for
the aggravation to which you are subjecting yourself. What can
you do to make your suffering easier to live with during this
time of transition? One of the most courageous examples of this
that I have ever witnessed was evidenced by a group of people
who had multiple sclerosis. They had gathered together to help
organize support groups for others who also had M.S. I had expected self-pity, resentment, anger, despondency, but I was surprised to discover that this was one of the most upbeat groups
of folks I had ever worked with. I even heard one man in a
motorized wheelchair say that he felt sorry for one of the able-
bodied spouses in attendance because she clearly was not living her life to the fullest. She was dead on her feet, but he was
trying to live every moment of his precious life to its fullest.
Pain had helped him take nothing for granted.

What gave this group of people the courage and resolve to
live with their suffering was their overriding sense of purpose:
they wanted to help others. It was because they had lived with

pain as a constant companion that they were in a position to understand what others were going through. They were elated with their sense of mission. They were excited that they were starting a movement. Why limit themselves to multiple sclerosis? They would reach out to all those in the area with any chronic illness.

I left that room full of people feeling utterly disabled myself. How dare I complain about how tough my life was, how intolerable my pain was, compared to the suffering that these folks had lived with! Surely if they could find some meaning in their painful existence, I could deal with the annoyances I put up with when somebody gave me a hard time, when I was upset over a conflict in my life.

Take the Hard Way Out

Anything in life that is worth doing is difficult. I believe this credo with all my heart. Given a choice between two possible courses of action, doing what you are already doing or doing something else, you probably are going to select what you are already doing. It is easy. You have had years of practice. Even if you know that you will encounter some aggravation, it is *predictable* pain. You have learned to live with it. You know exactly what to expect. If every day you walk through a door that you know will hit you on the head when it swings back, eventually you become accustomed to the pain. You are ready for it. No big deal. You get hit. Then it is over. But what if you don't walk through that door? What if you do something else? Initially, that may seem quite logical, but the reality is that most people prefer known pain to something that is unknown.

Joslyn could make this case quite easily: "Look, I know what to expect when I see James. He will treat me like crap, true, but at least there are no surprises. But if I end this relationship, then I will have to be alone. I will have to learn to live with myself. I may not have many conflicts in my life, but I will be very lonely. I like it better this way, where I deal with a pain that I know and can handle rather than one that may be too much for me."

"Take the hard way out" is a reminder that if you really ever want to change the ways you deal with people in your life, the ways you respond to conflict internally and externally, you will have to start taking on some new challenges, trading a familiar kind of pain for another that is far more threatening. But then, you don't have as much choice as you think.

When Discomfort Gets Out of Control

I do not mean to imply that we should worship pain, discomfort, conflict, and stress as wonderful opportunities for learning and growth. Yes, it is possible to gain something from even the most annoying, noxious circumstances. The problem, however, is that when people are living under such conditions, they tend to be more unreasonable, uncooperative, and irrational than they otherwise would be.

While discomfort may be harnessed for useful purposes, keep in mind that it also can be crippling. Relationships represent the best part of your life, some of the hours of greatest pleasure you will ever experience, and also the worst part, producing the most excruciating pain you have ever known. The wounds will never completely heal from adolescence when you were rejected by someone you really liked, when you were closed out of a group to which you badly wanted to belong, when you were teased or ridiculed by your peers. For those even more unfortunate souls, conflicts in peer relationships were dwarfed by the craziness that took place at home: parents fighting, emotional, even physical or sexual abuse taking place. The home was not so much a sanctuary as it was a battleground.

Years, even decades later, scar tissue still covers these wounds. That is why we are so wary and cautious in our relationships as adults, determined to never be that vulnerable again. Conflicts reminiscent of the distant past continue to plague us. Most of us still fight for approval from our parents, even after they are long dead. We still try to win acceptance among our peers. We still compete with our siblings and continue to harbor resentments toward those we believe were favored. No matter how long and hard we have been working at it, people still do not understand us or treat us with the respect we believe we deserve.

In conflict situations, discomfort may very well get out of control, to the point where judgment is clouded, decision making is impaired, and behavior is erratic. Both your conduct and that of your adversary become irrational and unpredictable in the midst of the stress that accompanies conflict. Extreme discomfort and stress interfere with people's ability to reason and distort their perceptions of events—exaggerating others' hostility and blaming them for wrongdoings. What makes conflict so dangerous is that opponents, who are each feeling the stresses and strains of hostile engagement, are experiencing the following symptoms:

Perceptual distortions. Stress creates hypervigilance, or the tendency to attend selectively to those signals that are perceived as threatening. In addition, people shut down their normal information-processing systems, distorting what they see and hear.

Memory deficits. During periods of stress, people are less able to recall accurately what transpired. Details about some aspects of the experience are ignored while others are "creatively" elaborated.

Dysfunctional beliefs. Stress leads to attitudes that are protective yet often counterproductive. People under stress are more negative and pessimistic in the ways they approach situations. They subscribe to beliefs that reinforce feelings of helplessness and vulnerability ("If I don't win this argument I will be forever humiliated.").

Physical symptoms. A wide assortment of physical consequences result from exposure to stress, including but not limited to hypertension, addictions such as smoking and alcohol and drug abuse, coronary problems, immunological or respiratory problems, asthma and allergies, digestive ailments, and sleep disturbances and other habit changes.

Emotional instability. People in conflict are prone to feelings of depression, anxiety, panic, and helplessness. As such, they are not in the ideal position from which to make intelligent reflective decisions, nor are they in optimal condition to take constructive action.

During the times of stress that undergird most interpersonal conflicts, you are less inclined than usual to attend to what an adversary is saying. You are more on guard, feeling defensive and provoked. The discomfort associated with conflict also distorts people's ability to see and hear things clearly. People in conflicted circumstances tend to ascribe (erroneously) to forces external to them the cause of the difficulty. They also are less able to deal with complexity in human interactions, tending to over-simplify what is taking place. Finally, in the heat of battle they become less articulate and less able to communicate persuasively.

The picture emerging here is that when we most need to be clearheaded, objective, and influential, conflict renders us less able to perform up to our normal capabilities. In addition, the greater the discomfort level you are experiencing, the more likely you are to attribute causes of conflict to someone or some-thing outside of yourself. Internal pressure must be reduced be-fore self-responsibility for problems will occur. In short, reason-ing abilities, cognitive capacities, and information processing will not operate properly without a certain degree of inner calm-ness in the face of perceived threats.

Understanding the patterns of conflict in your life will help you recognize the earliest signs of stress, with its correspond-ing decrease in personal functioning. Once you understand that your typical disagreements with others represent a lifelong strug-gle for you to maintain your own sense of potency, you may direct your efforts to taking yourself "off probation"—so that your very value as a human being is not contingent on saving face or conquering territory.

Putting Your Discomfort to Use

If only self-knowledge were enough. If only your understand-ing of past mistakes automatically led you to not repeat them. The reality is that there are many things in life that you are unwilling to change but about which you are very clear—that certain friendships don't meet your needs (but you stay in them anyway), that certain people should not be trusted (but you continue to do so), that you are much better off if you do not engage in certain behaviors (but you do them anyway).

One legitimate criticism leveled against educational programs, especially those that are therapeutic in their intent, is the difficulty of applying what has been learned outside the confines of the learning situation. How many people have you known who have been in therapy or counseling for years, who can articulate beautifully why they are so dysfunctional, but who do not seem to ever change? They may have tremendous insight into the causes and origins of their troubles. They have great depth of understanding into their unconscious motives and unresolved issues. But this self-knowledge is not applied or practiced in a meaningful way.

Real insight, if it is truly part of you, cannot really exist as mere intellectual revelations. People who are students of psychology, who have been in therapy for years, who can spout a dozen theories to explain why they are the way they are but who do not apply this knowledge effectively, cannot possibly lay claim to true wisdom. As the next chapter drives home, legitimate learning takes place only when you put your insights to work, when you take responsibility for your predicament without feeling the need to blame others.

CHAPTER FOUR

Taking Responsibility Without Blaming

Now THAT YOU ARE sufficiently uneasy with the ways you have handled conflicted relationships in your life, as well as with the core issues at the heart of your troubles, allowing yourself to feel uncomfortable can just as easily lead to more blame as to more action. The object of this stage in the process, therefore, is to learn to take responsibility for your less-than-satisfactory relationships—*without* blaming either yourself or anyone else for the predicament.

If you spent half as much time changing the ways you respond in conflict situations as you do trying to figure out who is at fault, most of your troubles would soon vanish. Most people are obsessed with identifying the culprit who is responsible for a dispute. On the one hand, if you can justify that it is *they* who were negligent or irresponsible, you may rub your hands together in glee and rest easy in the knowledge that at least you are not the one who created the mess, even if you do have to live with it. If, on the other hand, you frankly admit (or you are trapped into doing so) that *you*, not they, are responsible, then you can just as easily fall into the trap of feeling guilty and remorseful.

Since most of the time adversaries are not willing to accept blame, even when all evidence points toward them, it is largely a futile exercise trying to figure out who is at fault. Of course, it is helpful to determine the causes of disastrous situations for the purposes of not repeating the same mistakes and learning from these failures, but only when the focus is on enlightenment rather than on assigning guilt.

This distinction is especially important when you consider that interpersonal conflicts are almost always the consequence of collective efforts. Even if it were possible to discern who is at fault, what difference would it make? You are still both stuck with the problem.

Who Is to Blame?

In order to apply what you have learned from the previous stages in the process you must realize that determining who is at fault is an impossible task. The process described in this book requires that you identify who and what sets you off, understand the causes and origins of your entrenched patterns, and work through your discomfort until you are willing to accept greater responsibility for your troubles. You may not always be able to discover a single person or event that is causing your difficulties.

Conflicted relationships tend to perpetuate themselves, playing off interactions, carrying forward with a momentum that appears to have a life of its own. Any intention on the part of one person is predicated on the best prediction of what another person might do. If you are expecting a person to act deviously, you will prepare yourself for betrayal by cloaking your own behavior in deception. Conflicts are thus self-sustaining cycles of response and counterresponse, as illustrated in the following case of a mother- and daughter-in-law.

From the very beginning, Fran and Tina regarded one another with suspicion. Fran believed her son was making a mistake by getting married too young, and she channeled these feelings into resentment toward Tina (it is often easier to show disappointment or anger to a stranger than to a loved one). Tina, in turn, resented her mother-in-law for what she felt was excessive meddling. Each was convinced the other had ulterior motives for sabotaging her relationship with Brian, the son/husband. And, naturally, both were acting out a struggle that was a reenactment of something they had experienced before: Fran did not want her son to repeat the same mistakes she had made, and Tina had been so dominated by her own mother throughout much of her life that she was determined not to let this new mother control her life.

Tina held out an olive branch to her mother-in-law, inviting her to go to lunch one day. Fran, expecting some hidden agenda, accepted reluctantly and behaved with a certain amount of antagonism during the meal. Tina, perceiving her mother-in-law as ungrateful, launched her own defensive campaign, an attack that Fran was expecting and so interpreted as aggression on her part. When Brian heard the report that night from both combatants, each tried to convince him that the other was at fault for the conflict.

The central theme of this stage in the process, taking responsibility without blaming others or yourself, involves understanding the reciprocal nature of interpersonal difficulties. One of the most fascinating aspects of human behavior is that we do not always obey the laws of the physical world, at least with regard to what causes us to act. Whereas the laws of physics are based on a model of "linear causality," human behavior is best described as being based on "circular causality." What this means is that unlike the physical world, where it may be determined that one thing *causes* another, which in turn *causes* something else, human interactions are both causes *and* effects of what transpired previously.

This is as true for what is going on in your life now as it was for the circumstances of your past. At one time, I used to blame my mother for neglecting me, for instigating the continual arguments we had throughout my childhood and adolescence until I moved out at age seventeen. After all, she was an alcoholic. She was addicted to prescription tranquilizers, to food, to misery. When she died prematurely of cancer (and probably chronic depression), she provided me with the perfect scapegoat: it was *her* fault that I was continuously in conflict with other women in positions of authority.

Eventually, after studying the matter in depth over years of reflection, family research, journal writing, and therapy, I came to realize that my mother was only reacting to the forces of her own life—the ways she had been treated by her own parents, by my father, and even (it was difficult to admit) by my brothers and me. I realized that it was impossible to figure out who was at fault for the conflicts with my mother in the past, just as it is for those in the present.

It may appear as though a conflict results from a linear progression: I treat you disrespectfully because I am insensitive (or so you believe). Most situations are more complex: I felt slighted by you, even though you are unaware of this offense. I then approach you more tentatively in our next meeting, which you interpret as a lack of interest on my part. You begin to respond curtly, thereby reinforcing my feelings of rejection. I lash out next time, feeling totally justified but thereby appearing to be the one with the problem. You then innocently complain: "What is *his* problem?," never realizing your own role in the conflict. Most situations are even more complex than this since they involve more than two people.

You observe a family in action, for example. Thinking linearly, you see a child misbehaving, note that the parents argue between themselves before they decide what to do, and then, somewhat ineffectively, attempt to intervene to control their child. When you examine the situation in greater depth, you find that assigning blame is not as simple as you first thought. When the child misbehaves, his sister tattles to the mother, who promptly becomes angry. She then complains to the father, who punishes the child. The boy starts to pout and cry, sparking guilt in his sister, who got him in trouble. She then starts to act out herself, whining and complaining. The father and mother start arguing about whose fault this is. The boy then misbehaves again as a distraction, so his parents will stop fighting. The circular pattern continues round and round, each participant reacting to the other family members.

Who is at fault in this conflict? Is it the child who misbehaves? The sibling who manipulates the parents? The mother for being passive? The father for taking over? It is impossible to find the *single* source of this conflict, just as we cannot isolate who is causing whom to do what. All of their actions are interdependent, playing off of and reacting in response to each other's behavior. More often than not, circular causality is the most appropriate model for explaining what takes place during conflict situations.

The Introspective Process of Accepting Responsibility

Tanya and Samantha, two sisters who live in the same town, continuously bicker with one another over various imagined slights.

81

Tanya invites their parents over for dinner one night but decides not to include her sister and her family at the gathering. Samantha becomes indignant when she learns of it and vows not to include Tanya and her family the next time there is a holiday get-together.

So who is at fault in this situation: Tanya for not including her sister at the first dinner? Samantha for being so petty that she reciprocated in kind, thereby escalating the conflict? How about their parents for constantly comparing the two sisters? Each time one sister checks in with her parents, she hears an up-to-date summary of all the successes the other sister has enjoyed during the previous week.

Of course, whatever conflict exists between them has its roots in interactions that began long ago, during childhood. The sisters grew up in competition with each other—vying to be the one who could get the best grades, the most popular boyfriend, the most successful husband, the most promising career, the largest home, the fanciest car, the brightest children. Clearly, neither one of them is solely responsible for their long-standing conflicts. Nor is it relevant, at this juncture, to blame their parents for pitting them against one another, or at least failing to neutralize their mutual antagonism.

The conclusion as to who is at fault for any situation is thus predicated on answering these questions: Is anyone responsible for what happened? What is the cause of the conflict? Who is to blame? When a person is held responsible for an event, does that mean that he or she is at fault? What am I doing inside my own head to deny responsibility for what has been happening in an effort to place blame elsewhere?

These are the questions Tanya considered when she came

in to see me. She was sick and tired of enduring the constant strain in her relationship with Samantha. Was there anything she could do to stop the squabbles between them?

In order to break the blaming cycle in which each sister took turns finding fault with the other, collecting evidence to prove that the other one was to blame for the situation, it was necessary for Tanya to move away from such obsessive focus on what Samantha was up to and instead concentrate on what she could do to think more constructively about what was going on. This involved figuring out what button Samantha was pushing that elicited such resentment (the implication that she wasn't good enough), discovering where the origins of their struggles lay (a reenactment of their competition for their parents' approval), and harnessing her feelings of rejection and hurt as motivators to look inward rather than outward for the source of the difficulty.

Taking responsibility for the conflict does not mean blaming yourself instead of blaming the other person. Such a strategy can be just as counterproductive, sometimes even more so since it can involve a tendency toward self-pity and helplessness. At least when you are finding fault with others you are feeling feisty in the act of fighting back instead of withdrawing into a shell surrounded by the trophies of your failures.

Taking responsibility for the relationships in your life that are not going well without accepting blame for the troubles involves an internal process wherein you address a series of introspective inquiries. This procedure proved useful for Tanya in her efforts to regain more control over her perceptions of her sister and their relationship, even if she could not change their interactive patterns.

1. How Are You Disowning the Problem?

Notice the tendency to sidestep responsibility for what has happened before and what continues to take place in the conflicted relationship. For Tanya, this task proved to be quite easy with the assistance of her husband, who had listened far too long to her list of complaints.

"My husband pointed out to me how much time I spend thinking about my sister, bitching about what she is doing. He kids me that I may forget to make the kids' lunches, or to pick him up at the car dealership, but I have never forgotten a single episode of any injustice Samantha has inflicted on me. He is right. I do spend an inordinate amount of time denying that the problem between us is in any way my fault. Yet I can provide you with the longest list of reasons as to why I am so sure she is the one who is so unreasonable. I guess that only supports the argument that I am unwilling to take some responsibility for this mess."

2. In What Ways Are You Making Excuses for Yourself?

Part of the strategy for avoiding responsibility for the conflicts in your life is to construct a list of excuses, preferably as long as possible, that get you off the hook. If you are particularly bright, then you probably have developed especially good excuses that may not easily be discounted. Even if you are an amateur at this internal activity, it is likely that you have collected a list of favorites, such as:

I didn't do it.	I couldn't help it.
It was just dumb luck.	I didn't mean it.
I wasn't even there.	Don't look at me—she did it.

She asked for it.	Yes, but . . .
I didn't mean to do it.	Anyone would have done the same thing.
It wasn't my fault.	
I was just following orders.	She was asking for trouble.
I was just kidding.	I wasn't really trying.
It was just meant to be that way.	A bad temper runs in my family.
It wasn't me, it was the . . .	It was just an unfortunate situation.
It wasn't me, and I don't know who did it.	
It wasn't a big deal.	I didn't know the rules.
I had no choice.	Nobody told me.

Recall a time recently when someone leveled blame at you for something that you did. What was your initial response? Before you had time to even think through your role and responsibility, to reflect on your degree of culpability, the first excuse was already out of your mouth. Note, for instance, how this automatic defense works for a twelve-year-old boy who has been accused by his father of some alleged misdeed:

FATHER: I notice someone left the ice cream out all night.

SON: It wasn't me!

FATHER: There was nobody else home last night who had anything to eat.

SON: Maybe someone got up in the middle of the night and had a snack. Why do you always assume it is me?

FATHER: Are you saying that you didn't do it?

SON: I *may* have done it. I really don't remember.

FATHER: You don't remember?

85

SON: Okay. Big deal. So it was me. But it wasn't really my fault.

FATHER: No? Whose fault was it?

SON: Well, the phone rang when I was scooping the ice cream. And then you asked me to get something for you. Then I had to do my homework. I was preoccupied because I had too much to do.

FATHER: So now you are pleading mitigating circumstances.

SON: Excuse me?

FATHER: I was just saying that you admit you did it, but it wasn't your fault?

SON: Exactly! I mean, I didn't plan to do it. It is one of those things that just happened.

Almost every possible defense against an accusation is manifested in this dialogue between a parent and child. Under such circumstances, when a person is most interested in disowning responsibility for his or her behavior, the interaction becomes comical as well as extremely frustrating. These excuses are designed to maintain our good standing in the face of negative implications of our actions, and sometimes the stretch reaches ridiculous proportions.

Such is the mechanism of excuse making as a self-protection cloak. You remain safe from criticism and keep assaults to a fragile self-image at bay, but in the process you never take the opportunity to identify the triggers that provoked your defensiveness. You are not able to understand what it is within you that feels threatened and vulnerable, nor are you able to talk things through, with yourself and others, to prevent further distortions in the future.

In the preceding dialogue between a father and son, once they were able to put the issue of blame aside, they were able to sit down and discuss what their interaction was all about. The son explained that he felt constantly criticized by his father, that he could never measure up to his expectations. The father, aghast at this perception of himself, at first tried to make some excuses of his own. After recognizing that he was essentially doing the same thing that his son had been doing, circumventing responsibility, he began to look at his critical behavior and how it originated from his family of origin. Eventually, they were both able to learn a lot from this exchange over melting ice cream.

If facing conflict without blame presents such wonderful opportunities for growth, why don't we do this more often? The answer is that it takes a tremendous amount of work. If you can get away with an excuse that deflects blame away from you, initially you keep your image clear. You stave off, at least temporarily, any of the effort associated with having to make changes.

In an example from my own life, I made a joke to someone that was taken offensively. If it is true that I was insensitive when I made this joke, then that means I must (1) admit that I was wrong and still feel all right about myself, and (2) monitor myself more closely in the future so that I engage in more socially appropriate behavior. That is a lot of work.

If I choose to sidestep responsibility, however, I may avoid the effort involved in dealing with myself and others but I also miss an opportunity to become more effective. By sloughing off the joke incident as a case of the other person being "over-sensitive," or of me "just kidding," I do not learn anything from the experience, nor do I adjust my actions in the future.

Sometimes it feels so potent to be able to say, "I was wrong" or "It is my fault." It is empowering to acknowledge the truth: "Yes, I made a mistake. So?" This is thrown out not as a challenge, but as a demonstration of your own power. It takes a very secure and strong individual to be able to shoulder the consequences of mistakes without feeling personally threatened. Accepting partial responsibility diffuses blame and excuses on your own terms. What more is there to say about blame during a conflict after one person acknowledges her role in its creation? More often than not, such courage helps the other person reciprocate in kind: "Well, yeah, I appreciate your admitting that. I guess I got out of hand as well."

It is clearly a distortion of reality to deny your share of responsibility in *any* conflict. Even if you can convince someone you had no role in the disagreement (and that is doubtful), *you* know deep down inside that you are not totally blameless. Kidding yourself in one set of circumstances only leads to further self-deception in others. After a while, you will find it difficult to separate your fantasies about what is taking place from the actual objective events. In other words, you will believe your own lies and distortions, which further insulates you from receiving accurate information about the world and honest feedback about how you are perceived by others.

3. What Are Your Favorite Scapegoats for Diverting Blame Away from Yourself?

What are your favorite ways to divert attention and responsibility away from you and place it elsewhere? Is it poor genes? Bad luck? No support? A misunderstanding? Perhaps somebody else did it.

As with any self-respecting defense mechanism, blaming others for misdeeds allows you to maintain a positive self-image in light of attacks that are perceived as threatening. It buys you time until you can prepare a better excuse. It spreads around the focus of responsibility so that you do not bear the burden alone. Perhaps more important than rehabilitating your image in other people's eyes, blaming allows you to live with your own imperfections and still feel all right about yourself.

When a person is cornered into admitting that he or she did, in fact, do something, that it was intentional rather than accidental, and that he or she accepts responsibility for his or her actions, there is still a way to avoid blame: simply deny that there was anything wrong with what was done.

"Yes, you did tell me your concerns in confidence and ask me not to say anything to anyone else. Yes, I did promise I would honor your request. However, by keeping your feelings under wraps, by not confronting him with your concerns, by confiding in a few of us privately, you were only creating more divisiveness. I went to him and suggested that he approach you because I wanted the two of you to work things out. I felt an obligation not only to our relationship but also to the way we all get along."

Appealing to some greater good to explain one's actions is not the same as denying one's responsibility for creating a conflict. By offering a seemingly viable explanation, the individual accepts responsibility but denies any wrongdoing. The more comprehensible and rational the reasons, the more likely it is that he or she will not be held accountable.

Another means by which to disown responsibility is to *focus on the issue of intentionality:* you may have done it, but you did not mean to. This avoidance of blame goes something like this:

"There was no way I could have imagined that things would get this far out of control. I should not have been placed in this situation to begin with. I was just trying to be helpful."

A third possible response to an accusation is to imply that *you were coerced into acting this way.* You had no other choice; you were forced to do it.

"Hey, what would *you* have done? I could not risk doing anything else. I was in jeopardy, in such a vulnerable position that I was virtually forced to do it. I wish I could have acted otherwise, but there was just no other alternative."

Each of these denials of blame will only be employed when responsibility can be proven. Always the first choice is to *deny that you had anything to do with the situation in the first place.*

One of the best examples of using this type of excuse as a defense against blame comes from a favorite story of comedian Bill Cosby. It seems that one evening late at night, when Bill and his brother were supposed to be sleeping, they began wrestling around in bed. These tussles led to progressively more vigorous games, eventually culminating in "trampoline," in which they determined who could bounce the highest. When the bed came crashing down, the boys' father rushed into the room, ready to seek some revenge for his sleep being disrupted. "What is going on in here? Who broke this bed?"

Bill and his brother looked at one another. Even then showing signs that he was fast on his feet, Bill confidently proclaimed, "It was a robber! He came in through the window when we were sleeping. He woke us up jumping on the bed. Then he broke it! He escaped before we knew what happened."

"Son," his father calmly pointed out, "You don't have a window in this room. How could a robber come in through the window?"

Desperate to escape blame but never skipping a beat, Bill replied, "Well, Dad, he took it with him."

The lengths people will go to to avoid responsibility are indeed humorous. If only blaming others did not have such dangerous side effects. For when you believe that your troubles are the result of what someone or something else is doing to you, you are powerless to stop them. Your only recourses are to duck, endure, or get out of the way.

It is apparent that people are most likely to blame others for their misfortunes under the following circumstances:

- When someone else is present (such as in all interpersonal conflicts)
- When the other person involved in the conflict is in a higher position of power or authority (boss, parent, and so on)
- When the other person is disliked or not respected
- When the outcome is severe
- When people are unaware that the patterns of their conflicts are replications of unresolved issues from the past

It is counterproductive to blame others, but it can be just as destructive to blame yourself for unpleasant circumstances. Rather than dwelling on who is at fault, it is far better for you to accept responsibility for overcoming the problem and get on with the business of taking charge of this process and working things through. This effort is easier said than done, for the chief obstacles that get in the way of resolving conflicts are those unresolved issues that you have been ignoring.

4. What Might I Do Internally to Feel More in Control Over What Happens Externally?

The consequence of accepting responsibility for a conflict is that you then have to do a tremendous amount of work on yourself in order to rectify matters. This has a lot less to do with things you do on the outside than with internal strategies you can adopt to feel more personal control and take responsibility for your internal feelings.

Attributing blame for conflict to someone or something outside of yourself represents a gross distortion of reality. Cognitive therapists (so called because they emphasize changing internal thinking patterns) have been writing for decades about the irrational beliefs people subscribe to that insist that feelings are reactions *caused* by what other people do:

"You *make* me so angry." (implying that the other person did something that created this feeling)

"You *made* me do it!" (insinuating that what the other person did necessarily caused this person's response)

"Why did you do that *to* me?" (signifying that the other person's actions were deliberately directed toward the speaker)

"If it were not for you . . ." (implying that if the other person did not exist, this person would not have any problems)

Actually, interpersonal struggles involve more than just one's chosen reaction to what has taken place. Certainly cognitive activity—that is, one's interpretation of others' actions—does influence how he or she feels about and responds to them. But in

92

a complicated interaction between two people, individuals often trigger reactions in one another not only through their present behavior but through their unresolved issues as well.

When you attempt to assign blame for a problem, you are likely to follow one of three possible scenarios, none of which is strictly accurate.

1. *External blame:* "It is all your fault. If only you were different, then we would not have this problem between us."
2. *Scapegoat:* "We got manipulated into this conflict. If they had handled things differently, then you and I would not be having this problem."

Both of the above cognitive styles attribute blame to circumstances outside your control. You bear little responsibility for the situation, and so you have little power to change it. In the third case, you take total responsibility for the conflict.

3. *Internal blame:* "It *is* my fault. If I had reacted differently, then we would not be in this mess."

This is also a distortion of reality, since it is highly unlikely that anything is ever entirely one person's fault. Nevertheless, given a choice among the three blaming strategies, even with the remorse and guilt that accompany self-blame, this is still a more empowering way to think about your plight. At the very least, you are implying that you *choose* your reaction to what happened, meaning that you still can choose to think or act in a way that will produce a different reaction. Such personal responsibility is only possible, however, when you avoid the tendency to make excuses.

Counteracting External Blame

It is virtually a requirement for resolving any conflict that both adversaries must share responsibility for its continuation or its resolution. Since you cannot force someone else to do or think something they do not wish to, since you cannot patch up a dispute by yourself, the first and most useful direction for your attention ought to be to reclaim your own power. Ironically, the quickest way to dispel feelings of helplessness is to acknowledge your own role in creating the problem. As long as your troubles are other people's fault, you have no choice but to wait for them to see the error of their ways. If, however, you acknowledge the interactive nature of conflict and recognize what you have done, and are presently doing, to keep the struggle going, you then have choices about what you might do differently.

There is no more vulnerable feeling than the *perception* that something is being done to you against your will. It is far better to look inward rather than outward for the problem and the solution. This works, however, only when you can take the heat, a prospect that will seem formidable indeed unless you have fortified your own internal strength.

Bolstering Self-esteem

If you can accept yourself as flawed and imperfect, as sometimes doing and saying stupid things, and still maintain a sense that you are basically a good person, then it is not so threatening to say "I'm wrong." You can afford to take some heat because the security of your core is not at stake, even though it sometimes feels that way.

During your inward journey, you will notice certain inclinations and predispositions to tear yourself down (and thereby

94

decrease the internal strength you have to face conflicts more directly). This tendency comes from several sources, most of which you are in a position to alter if you so choose. Most notably, certain unrealistic attitudes you hold will consistently get you into trouble, such as the following:

- That you are perfectly fluid and graceful in everything you try, even the first time. *When he brought up that stuff from the past, I should have seen it coming. I know that I had never been in that position of responsibility before, but still, I should have been able to adapt more quickly. Then when things started to unravel, I should have anticipated better what would happen next. I seriously question whether I should even be in this position. Why did they promote me so quickly? It is their fault for putting me in a role for which I am not prepared.*

- That you will be successful all of the time. *I don't know how many times I rehearsed what I would say once we were alone. I have been in similar situations dozens of times before, and I have always handled the conflict without losing my cool. All I had to do was follow my plan, but no, I had to try and fix the whole mess. I guess I am not cut out for this kind of relationship. I probably don't even deserve it.*

- That when you do not meet your standards of perfection, it is because you have discovered evidence that deep down inside you are really a fraud. *I knew it! I knew it all along! How could I have let myself think that this time things would be different? I don't know why I even bother trying any more. No matter what I do, or how hard I try, I am still going to get what I deserve—nothing. This is just another example that proves that I am just pulling the wool over other people's eyes. The ones who can see what is underneath realize only too well that I am not worth the effort.*

These self-defeating attitudes are pervasive in your internal dialogues during times when you feel most distraught over a conflict in your life. If you are not busy reciting a list of excuses for why things should be different, or finding fault with others who have made your life unnecessarily uncomfortable, then you are probably taking big chunks out of your own self-esteem through your unrealistic expectations. These distortions and exaggerations that take place inside you may be counteracted by reminding yourself that:

- *Just because I prefer things to happen a certain way does not mean I need them to be so in order to function effectively.*
- *No matter how hard I try and how badly I would like to be even more skilled and accomplished in what I do, I will still come up short of what I want.*
- *Just because I make mistakes and occasionally fail to do what I want, it does not make me a failure as a person.*

Fear of Failure

Another characteristic you may find when you look inward is a systematic series of defenses designed to protect you from facing your imperfections and flaws. Most often appearing in the form of rationalizations, they involve constructing elaborate excuses to deny your role in a conflict.

Throughout my life I have been obsessed with failure, so much so that I coauthored a book on the subject. I had hoped that by interviewing accomplished practitioners of my profession, asking them about their experiences with failure in life, I would feel better about my own lapses. You see, in life, we often only talk about success. We may broadcast to all the world instances of our victories—promotions at work, conquests in relationships, arguments in which we prevailed, winnings at the gambling tables—but rarely will we talk about disappointments and failures.

In training to be a therapist, for example, all we were ever exposed to were demonstrations of perfection. Our professors and supervisors related numerous stories in which seemingly hopeless cases were cured by their brilliant interventions. We observed videos of the great masters doing therapy, conducting perfect sessions in which they helped an individual resolve a lifelong struggle and still saved a few minutes at the end of the half hour to explain how and why they were so effective. All the cases we read about in our texts involved incredibly complex situations in which the author knew exactly what to do and then did it quite smoothly.

As beginners, we compared our experiences to those of our mentors. I felt awkward and confused much of the time. Often I did not know what to do with my clients, and even when I did know, I could not do it as well as I would have liked. Yet I could not talk about these cases. It was not safe to admit that I did not know what to do. During group supervision sessions, it became the norm to bring up only those cases in which you already knew what was going on; that way you could defend yourself properly. The object was to keep away any inkling that we were somehow deficient.

I have since learned that my experience was not unique.

Not only in the practice of therapy, but in virtually every field it is not acceptable to admit that you do not know what you are doing. You must pretend that you are perfectly competent in everything you do. And if you do not feel that way, fake it. If you do not believe this, imagine how you would react if your doctor, lawyer, or car mechanic were honest with you and told you: "I don't have any idea what is going on. But stick with me, and maybe I can figure something out."

When you are able to come to terms with your own imperfections and faults, when you can readily accept the fact that sometimes you fail but it does not make you a failure, then, only then, can you embrace mistakes as opportunities for learning. Yes, you heard me correctly: *embrace* failure as potentially growthful. Think of failure as constructive feedback telling you that something you tried did not work. Feel grateful for the clarity of the message so that you do not repeat the same mistakes. Allow your misjudgments to help you be more flexible in the future, more determined to improve your effectiveness. Forgive yourself for being imperfect. Treat failures as merely useful information about what works and what does not.

The Need for Internal Control

I will sometimes take the need to feel in control over my life to such great lengths that even when something happens that clearly has nothing to do with my actions, I will still find a way to feel responsible. I engage in this magical thinking not because I am a glutton for punishment but because I enjoy the feeling that things are not done *to* me without my participation and consent.

A store clerk, whom I have never met in my life, yells at

me because I was too slow advancing in the line. (This was not the case.) All the while I recognize that this lady is having a bad day, or maybe she is not a very nice person. I also begin to look at what I might have done, even oh so subtly and unconsciously, to invite this abuse. Do I project an air of "kick me?" What is it about my appearance, or the way I present myself, that encouraged her to lash out at me?

Now I realize, of course, that I take this internal control business to an extreme. Events of the world sometimes fall upon all of us simply because we are occupying a certain space at a particular moment. But I so like the feeling that what happens to me is a direct or indirect result of what I do that I prefer to assume first that I am partially to blame.

That does not make me an easy mark to take advantage of, for I may not tell *you* what I am doing. I may even try to make you believe that you are solely at fault for our conflict, but inside my own head, where it really counts, I am searching furiously for my role in the struggle.

The Search for Excuses

Before you can take back your power you must first be able to recognize that you are giving it away. This involves catching yourself in the act of trying to place blame elsewhere. Staying within the boundaries of reality—engaging in neither excessive self-blame nor excuse making—can help you discover the specific ways that you attempt to externalize responsibility.

By way of review, the excuses that are commonly used fall into four main groups: (1) "I didn't do it." (2) "I didn't mean to do it." (3) "They made me do it." and (4) "I couldn't help it." Monitor the dialogue going on inside your head anticipating, during, and after an argument. When you hear variations of the themes "That's not fair!" "How dare she do that *to* me!," "I didn't do anything! Why pick on me?," and "It wasn't my fault," it is likely that you are in an excuse-making mode.

When you listen to yourself during a heated exchange (a skill that requires tremendous resolve), you will notice a marked tendency to try and score points or land punches by trying to get the other person to admit that he is at fault and you are not. This almost never works.

Augmenting Options in Other Arenas

Relying on excuses and blaming others are acts of desperation. If you had other options, both internally and external strategies such as being assertive, debating convincingly, mediating, compromising—methods designed to negotiate outcomes that are satisfying to both participants—you would find them much more effective in settling disputes. Before experimenting with alternative means by which to deal with conflict, you must first commit yourself to action. As you will find in the next stage of the process, described in Chapter Five, this is not as easy as it sounds.

Committing Yourself to Act Differently

Now THAT YOU HAVE some idea about the patterns of conflict that have existed in your life, the big question is what do you intend to do about them?

Changing any lifelong pattern, especially one that is so ingrained in your interpersonal style, is a formidable task indeed. Before you can even begin to move into the realm of action, you must first decide that you are willing to invest the necessary time and energy and to take the risks that are involved in changing. I suggest you think long and hard about this choice before you make it—the consequences will be quite profound.

As much as you might not enjoy the discomfort that accompanies the ways you usually deal with conflict, I have mentioned that it is a kind of pain that is familiar to you. If you have become used to tolerating a certain amount of discord, humiliation, tension, and abuse, they become like old compatriots that you have learned to live with. That is the paradox of making personal changes: as much as you may want things to be different, you also like things the way they are. You have settled into a routine in which you know what to expect and you don't experience tremendous disappointment.

Imagine that things were different. At first, you might believe that all is well and you will live happily ever after. No longer do you respond in the same maladaptive ways, nor do you beat yourself up over mistakes and misjudgments. But think again. You also have to learn a whole new repertoire of skills in order to act differently. That takes a lot of work. When it comes right down to it, and people realize how much energy and commitment it takes to become more fully functioning, many prefer the familiar pain they are used to.

As you have already learned, the one thing that you have going for you the most is your own pain. One of the consequences of true insight is that you can no longer do the same things the same way without feeling even worse. If you *know* that the reason you have become unreasonable and rigid during an interaction is because it feels like your feelings were hurt, it is harder to get away with pouting—your games have become more explicit.

The key, then, to putting your insights to work and committing yourself to act differently is allowing your discomfort to help motivate you to take charge of the way your relationships are going. When you cannot change the interactions themselves, the next best choice is at least to take control of your own internal reactions. If in the future you start to feel bad every time you resort to previous patterns, you will no longer stay the same. You will change because you have no choice.

Moving Closer to Commitment

As with every component of the program described in this book, the stage of the process dealing with commitment to act differently involves a series of sequential steps, each naturally leading to the next. You will observe this process in action in the following vignette. As we follow this case through the process of commitment to action, you may find it instructive to apply what we are doing to your own conflicted relationships.

Daniel feels ambivalent about changing a few of his relationships—with his father, to whom he relates on a superficial level; with his wife, with whom he has negotiated a kind of truce in which they live together more as friends than as lovers; and with his mentor at work, with whom he is so deferential that he has lost his own identity. Sure, Daniel would like it if he and his father became closer, if he and his wife became more intimate, and if he and his mentor developed a more equal relationship. It is not the outcome that Daniel feels uncertain about: it is what he would have to do to initiate the changes that would make a difference. He has been through this process before, and he knows that the journey he would have to take involves uncovering and dealing with some of his unresolved issues from the past, with all the accompanying pain. "Maybe things aren't so bad after all," Daniel tells himself. He realizes all too well that in order to improve his relationships he would have to reach deep inside himself for the courage to not only commit himself to act differently but also follow through on his resolve.

Daniel's vacillation about whether to take the leap to confront the emptiness in his life or leave well enough alone eventually landed him in my office. He was confused, inconsistent from one moment to the next, and unable to commit himself to do much of anything. He even left it up to me to decide whether he would attend therapy to work his problems through: "What do *you* think?," he asked me in a tiny voice filled with uncertainty. "What should I do?"

I shrugged. Heck if I was going to bail him out. When I asked him whether he wanted to return for another session to begin working on his fear of commitment, he shrugged back at me, unwilling to commit himself to even that decision. Finally, after a silence that seemed to go on for several hours but probably lasted only a few long minutes, Daniel sighed with resignation. "Okay. Where do we begin?"

Creating an Image of What You Want

Given the anguish, the disappointment, the setbacks that are an integral part of making any significant life change, you will need a place you can go for recuperation and inspiration. That place does not exist in your neighborhood, or even on this planet; it is an image inside your own mind. This is the picture you create of the future, a time in which you no longer resort to ineffectual responses or torturous, self-demeaning acts. You can imagine yourself at a time in the not-too-distant future in which you are no longer perturbed by what a few others are doing. Likewise, you can picture yourself, really *see* yourself, responding differently to crisis situations that ordinarily might have sent you into a frenzy. You appear more in control, more self-assured and in charge of what you are doing, what you are thinking, and what you are feeling inside.

As you imagine your nemesis engaging in the usual manipulative ploys, deceitful actions, and insensitive behaviors, rather than becoming defensive or irritated as you normally would, you have at your disposal a wide-ranging assortment of strategies that you can employ effectively to keep the other person off your case. More importantly, you note that you have the power and the ability to keep yourself calm and in control.

As the preceding description made obvious, Daniel was most reluctant to take a stand on any aspect of his present, much less the future. Nevertheless, with some gentle prodding and encouragement on my part (yes, a bit of vigorous confrontation of his passivity as well), Daniel found that he was able to conjure an image of the way he would like his relationships to be. This was not easy for him because, on some level, he did not feel deserving of a life relatively free of significant conflict. His resistance to making changes came, in part, from never having experienced an existence that was conflict free. It was difficult for him to even fantasize a time in which things could be different from the way they were. It was all he had ever known.

It took several weeks for Daniel to give himself permission to complete this assignment. Every time he attempted to create an image of what he wanted, some scolding voice would interrupt or interference like that of fuzzy television reception would block his view. He stuck with the task, however, realizing that his relationships would never change unless he could first imagine that such progress was possible.

"I see myself at work. There is some pressure project that I am working on. There I am in my office. The door is shut. My feet are propped on the desk. I am staring out the window, utterly stuck as to what I will do. I reach for the phone. I am about to call Sandy, my mentor, to see if I can talk to him for a few minutes to run something by him. I know how this usually goes: I tell Sandy what I want to do. He tells me to do something else. I trust his judgment more than my own. I end up resenting him for that. We usually end up arguing and I always lose. He prevails on me to defer to his greater experience.

"This time, though, I don't call him. Instead I make a decision, *any* decision; it really doesn't matter what I decide, just so long as *I* am the one who makes the choice. I feel good about taking a stand on my own. Only afterward do I tell Sandy. He, of course, cuts me down for not consulting him. I don't blame him for that—he believes that he is just trying to help me. *I* am the one who relinquished my power and lost my identity to him.

"This time I don't become defensive when he attacks me. Neither do I become angry. I just calmly listen to him and tell him that I appreciate his help, but that I am trying to do more things on my own. He, of course, does not understand. *The important thing in this image is that I don't need him to understand in order for me to feel good about what I did.*

"I come home from work later that day. My wife asks me in a perfunctory way how my day was. This time, instead of giving her an answer just to put her off, I ask her if she will sit down with me for a few minutes as I want to tell her all the things that I am feeling and thinking. She is shocked and so complies with my request out of curiosity. This has never happened before. But in this image I can actually picture myself telling her about what happened, what I am trying to do, what I am feeling and thinking, the changes I am planning for the future.

"Since I am trying to make this as realistic as possible, she does not hug me with joy. How can I expect that after all these years of mutual neglect? So she picks a fight. Maybe she is afraid of getting close to me, too. Anyway, she ignores what I told her and tells me that I am stupid to jeopardize my relationship with Sandy just to exercise my macho need for control.

"Amazingly, I don't respond. I just nod calmly. Actually, I kind of used a few of the things that you do with me: you know—where you feed back to me what you heard me say? Rather than fighting back, I just reflect back to her the feelings of neglect and hurt that I can sense she is feeling. I suppose I have always been aware of these feelings, but I was unable to acknowledge them. Except in this image, I have just been too scared to let myself think about responding any differently."

Daniel was jubilant over his ability to picture himself responding differently to his mentor and to his wife. At this point, he could not yet bring himself to include his father, a figure in his life who was even more threatening. That is just fine, I told him. Let's start with these relationships. Later he could apply what he learned to others that seemed more challenging.

Daniel rehearsed this image several times a day. He would play with the scenarios, changing a few details here and there but staying with the same basic plot. In each case, he would imagine himself feeling and acting differently in response to what others would do to incite him. When he was feeling particularly good, he would further imagine himself initiating more in these relationships rather than only responding to what they offered to him. Pretty soon, he was able to incorporate this picture of himself as a decision maker and risk taker into his previous self-image, which was now in the process of becoming obsolete.

Facing the Consequences of Action

Creating images of the way you would like your relationships to be is not only cause for celebration—there are also consequences to getting this ball rolling. That is why Daniel was so reluctant to entertain fantasies of the future. He knew that once he started thinking about a different life, he would be spoiled forever. No longer could he pretend that being in conflict was acceptable once he had a taste, albeit in fantasy, of a different alternative.

If you let yourself imagine that in your primary conflicted relationship you no longer act the way you usually do, you will have little choice but to face the consequences of this rehearsed image. Like Daniel, now that you can imagine that you have other alternatives in how you respond to conflict, both internally and externally, you will feel even more uneasy at the prospect of staying vulnerable and dissatisfied. The image you have created of yourself as a more powerful being becomes like a cancer. It grows. It infects your whole spirit. It whispers to you constantly as you engage in the same old arguments: "You don't have to act this way. You do have other choices. Remember me, your image of the way you would like to be? What is stopping you from making that fantasy a reality?"

The only thing that stops you from putting your plan into action is your own inertia. This is the point at which Daniel encountered the most trouble of all. It was one thing for him to imagine himself acting differently; it was quite another to actually follow through on this commitment.

"Do you have any idea of what would happen if I actually said some of these things to Sandy or my wife? They would think I am nuts. Even worse, they would probably just write me off completely. I just can't risk it."

I pressed him further. "So let's follow through on what would happen if you were to act as you do in your fantasy. Don't be kind. Picture the worst possible scenario."

He needed less than a few seconds to answer. "Simple. Sandy

gets me fired for insubordination. The truce with my wife falls apart and we get a divorce. When I try to deal with my father on anything but a superficial level, he becomes indignant and won't speak to me anymore." He smiled smugly as if to say to me: "Ok, smartass, see if you can talk me into it now."

I refused to take the bait. "Okay, you win. You get to stay in these mediocre relationships in which conflict prevails. Now what do you want to do?" I smiled right back at him, knowing that he was already hooked on his image of a different way of being. He could never go back to the way he was.

"I just don't know what to do. I can't let things stay the way they are, but I can't risk letting things get out of hand." His pain was so palpable I was unwilling to just let him blow in the wind.

"Daniel, you have created the worst possible scenario. Your mentor fires you. Your wife leaves you. Your father never speaks to you. What you seem to be saying is that the only way people will stay involved with you is if you live up to what you believe are their expectations. If Sandy is really so intolerant of your need for independence, then I guess he isn't much of a mentor—whose role, by definition, is to help you find your own way. If the only way you can keep your marriage together is to avoid any semblance of intimacy, then you don't really have a marital partner; you have a roommate. If that is the case, I am certain you could find another roommate with whom you don't fight so much. As for your father, if he cannot sustain a relationship with you in which real feelings are expressed, in which you make contact on a personal level, and if he is unwilling to speak with you except on his terms, then perhaps it is best that you spend some time apart."

I could tell that he remained unconvinced. But at least now

he was examining the extent to which his predicted consequences were reasonable. He finally understood that perhaps
the results he imagined were not so awful after all. Certainly,
things would be terribly stressful in the short run—he would
have to find a new job, recruit a new mentor, go through a
divorce, be cut off from his father—but in the long run taking
action was the only way he could ever extricate himself from
the conflicts that were wearing him down.

Increasing Your Personal Resolve

You know what you need to do, but you feel this choking sen-
sation at the prospect of doing it. Every time you bring to mind
this picture of the new way you manage conflict, another more
morbid image engulfs both it and you like a voracious shark.
How dare you even imagine that you can break years of habitu-
ated action? Who are you kidding?

Even the best intentions toward commitment to action melt
away when you anticipate that things could be worse than they
presently are. This was the most inhibiting force within Daniel,
and it stymied his efforts to change long-standing patterns. In
an effort to help him increase his resolve, several strategies were
implemented that proved helpful.

1. *Stop focusing on the negative.* As long as you attend to
   everything that can go wrong rather than focusing on
   what can go quite smoothly, you will continue to
   frighten yourself into avoiding action. Daniel came into
   each session obsessed with the possibilities of disaster.
   He spent most of his time talking about what it would
   mean if bad things happened. We broke this cycle by

instituting a rule that in subsequent meetings we would only talk about the positive implications of his decisions. Likewise, you will find it much more inspiring if you force yourself to consider what could go wrong but then concentrate on the positive image of the future you created earlier.

2. *Remind yourself what you are doing and why.* Do not let yourself forget what is at stake. The fear that accompanies venturing into the unknown is a lot more tolerable when you firmly believe that the discomfort you are suffering is only part of the journey. All adventures have their inconveniences, trials, and tribulations.

3. *Putting a support system in place.* Your efforts to make significant changes in the ways you relate to others and yourself do not seem quite so overwhelming when you have surrounded yourself with people in whom you can trust. Especially when attempting to resolve conflicts, with all the emotional turmoil that is likely, it is much easier if you are not alone. You need people to confide in, to test out your plans, to help you live through the tough times when all does not go as you had anticipated.

Making a Public Commitment

A support system is useful not only to bounce ideas off of but, more simply, to hear out loud your commitment to act differently. It is much more difficult to back out of a promise when others have heard what you intend to do. It is one thing to tell yourself what you want to do; it is quite another to tell others who you know will monitor your progress. That is the appeal of weight loss programs such as Weight Watchers and substance

111

abuse programs such as Alcoholics Anonymous: tell somebody else that you plan to act differently, and you disappoint more than yourself if you change your mind. You also have to face the inquiries of those who have heard your commitment.

One of the simplest strategies I have used in my graduate classes when introducing the importance of public commitment in helping people change lifelong patterns is to ask the students to think of some relationship in their lives that they would wish to alter. Then I ask them to think of something that they might do differently in the future that would be a small step toward reducing the tension in that relationship. The next—and most important—step (besides actually making the change) is to tell their peers exactly what they will do in the coming week. What will they do? When will they do it? What will they do if they find themselves avoiding action?

It is understood that the next week each person will report to the rest of the students what they accomplished. The victory is *not* defined in terms of producing a positive outcome or a happy ending in which everything went as planned. Rather, the success comes from trying, from doing what they committed themselves to do.

I learned this lesson early in life. Actually, I was nineteen. I had spent most of adolescence roaming the shopping mall with my best friend, ostensibly to pick up girls. At one point, we had gone over forty Saturday afternoons in a row without missing a single opportunity. The amazing thing is that in all those hundreds of hours, we never once even approached girls, much less ever asked them out. We had our routine down to a science. Whenever two girls would walk within our range, we would argue furiously about which one of us would get the short one, which the tall one, or which the blonde and which the brunette. We would argue just long enough so that by the time we had made a decision, the girls would be nowhere to be found. I wasted my whole adolescence wanting to take risks but never doing so.

So there I was, nineteen years old, sitting with my family in a restaurant. It had always been my life's ambition to be old enough to ask out a waitress. Waitresses were goddesses to me. They were tall, or at least they always looked statuesque from where I sat. They seemed in charge of their turf, bubbly, high spirited. And they brought food!

I resolved then and there to ask one out. There wasn't that much to be afraid of. After all, nobody could hurt me as much as I did when I beat myself up over my refusal to take a risk. I told my family what I intended to do. There was no way I could back out now. I approached the first waitress, asked her out, and was unceremoniously refused. Hey, no problem. I went up to the next waitress and asked her out, too. She also turned me down. Strangely, rather than feeling rejected, I was feeling exhilarated with the power of knowing that nobody could ever reject me again. They could turn down the opportunity to be with me, but only I could decide to feel rejected. I therefore approached a third waitress, who was kind and told me she had a boyfriend. No matter. I had followed through on what I had said I would do. My victory was in the effort, not in the result.

Committing myself aloud to others helped bolster my resolve. I had wanted to crawl back into my shell, to think about how much I wished things could be different, to blame my inaction on circumstances outside of my control. But I would have to face them all afterwards, these people who knew. I felt that

I had no choice but to follow through on what I had said I would do.

I have never forgotten that day. I learned during my encounter with the three waitresses that I did have the courage to change. Nobody could hurt me as much as I hurt myself when I don't do what I say I will.

What about you? What have *you* been putting off? What excuses have you given yourself for accepting conflict in your relationships without changing the ways you deal with them? Who could you make a commitment to who could monitor your progress? Take some time out and make a plan.

Getting Ready. Set. Go.

Are you still here? You are not out there putting your plan into action? That's all right. In between commitment and action there is still a bit of planning to do. Now that you have said what you are going to do differently, you must figure out how you can best carry out your intentions.

Daniel spent considerable time with this step in the process, and not just to stall for time. He genuinely wanted to give himself the best possible shot at making his relationships work. He had prepared himself for the worst possible scenario, was even ready to accept the consequences of disappointing results; but if there was anything he could do to make things work out, he wanted to try his hardest.

Daniel became a student not only of himself but also of the others with whom he was connected in conflict. What was it about Sandy, his mentor, that made him need to control Daniel so thoroughly? What was it about Daniel that Sandy found so threatening? As for his wife, why was she so reluctant about getting closer to him? There had been a time when she had begged for just this reaction in him. Had she given up? Was she punishing him? Maybe she was just as frightened as he was. Finally, Daniel mused about the behavior of his father. Perhaps he was asking something of him for which he was wholly unprepared. His father had always been this way, and not just with him—with everyone.

The questions that Daniel began asking himself about his relationships were not merely introspective dialogues. He began talking to others as a way to prepare himself for the action that was soon to come. At times, he even broached the subjects with the targets themselves: "Sandy, I notice that when I express my own opinion about something and it differs from yours, you try to get me to change my mind rather than listening to what I have to say."

Daniel continued to test the water a bit, this time checking out his wife in a direct yet nonconfrontational manner: "Honey, just a moment ago I sat next to you on the couch and you moved over and then left the room. What might I be doing to drive you away?"

And with his father, Daniel tried to expand the boundaries a bit during their next conversation: "Dad, if we could put the basketball game aside for a moment, there is something I want to ask you. When I told you a few minutes ago that I was excited about the changes that I was making, you acted like you didn't even hear me. I was wondering what you thought about what I said?"

Of course, in each of these encounters, the people did not exactly jump for joy at Daniel's changed behavior. If anything, they thought he was acting a little weird, and they told him so. At this juncture, that was fine with him. He had been preparing himself not to expect much in the beginning. It had taken a long time for these relationships to develop into conflicted, dysfunctional encounters; he would not be able to change things overnight. But he *had* demonstrated that he was indeed capable of pushing the limits of what had been established previously. He was ready to take some risks.

Taking Risks

There is no way to skip this step. This is the part where your heart beats so hard it seems it will leap out of your chest, where when you even think about what you are going to do you can feel your resolve waver just as your knees buckle. All those excuses that you have so carefully formulated over the years come back at the feeblest invitation. "Hey, it isn't really so bad the way it is. You don't have to do this. Nobody is making you. Why not just put all this change stuff aside and do something really fun?"

The strange thing is that with practice taking risks becomes fun, perhaps the greatest kick life has to offer. Have you ever wondered what is the appeal of gambling, or risking injury skiing or driving fast or skydiving? Have you considered what is so captivating about watching a horror movie in which you know you are going to be subjected to unimagined misery before the lights come on again? Have you thought about why you sometimes do stupid things for no other reason than that it seemed like a good idea at the time? In each of these examples, the intent is to speed up your heartbeat, to experience life more intently, to immerse yourself so completely in life that time stands still while you complete your ride.

Now think about the prospect of confronting your nemesis. Consider what it would be like to act differently in conflict situations. Picture yourself stubbornly refusing to do the same old things and instead doing something quite out of character. These are risks every bit as exhilarating as riding on a roller coaster, hurtling a rubber raft down a rapid, or riding your luck on the roll of the dice. Risk taking becomes fun when you recognize that what you are about to do is more exciting than frightening, that you have a safety net in place to protect yourself from becoming severely injured, and that you are about to experience the ride of your life.

This is exactly what Daniel reminded himself of as he sat in Sandy's office, rehearsing in his head one more time what he wanted to say. As is sometimes the case, the conversation turned out so differently from what he had imagined. Rather than responding in his usual controlling, cynical way, Sandy became quiet and pensive. He did not react right away, and when he finally did speak, it was clear that he had not really heard what Daniel had said to him.

That was fine, Daniel thought. Actually, he felt kind of sad. He had placed Sandy on a pedestal, deified him in such a way that he had refused to acknowledge his limitations. Daniel was later to go through a stage in which he blamed Sandy for misleading him, but the fact of the matter was that nobody was at fault. It was simply time for Daniel to move on; he had outgrown what Sandy had to offer him. There was no reason for them to stay in conflict once they established positions on a more equal footing. This interaction pattern changed not so much through actions that Daniel took in his encounters with Sandy as through his internal decision to no longer defer to him at the expense of his own identity. A change in behavior soon followed the internal resolve.

The situation with his wife proved to be somewhat more challenging, a not-unexpected situation considering how long-standing their conflicts had been. Daniel continued the plan he had begun during his preparation process. At every opportunity, he attempted to engage his wife in honest dialogue. Since he could not control her moods or her willingness to reciprocate in kind, Daniel decided to commit himself to follow through only on that part of the interaction that was within his power—his own behavior. In his mind, he counseled himself to remain patient, to avoid blaming his wife since he, in fact, had "trained" her to be so self-protective. Likewise, he worked hard to avoid blaming himself for their stalemate.

On the outside, Daniel forced himself to keep attempting intimacy with his wife, even when she appeared to reject his efforts. I told him the story of my years at the mall and about my own realization that rejection was much more a state of mind than an actual circumstance. That seemed to fit quite well for him as well, for he started to feel proud of what he was doing even though his wife had responded minimally to his efforts. Again he reminded himself to be patient, to keep experimenting with different alternatives until he discovered a strategy that worked.

I would like to be able to tell you that this story has a happy ending. In a way, it does even though the marriage did not survive. It became apparent that both spouses had harbored resentments too long, had blamed one another so vigorously that the damage appeared irreparable. They moved in different directions after the divorce—his wife soon remarried, while Daniel spent some time alone before he was willing to risk again. The part he felt best about was that finally he and his now ex-wife were able to relate to one another without conflict.

Daniel was able to take what he learned from this marriage and apply it to other relationships in his life, most notably with his father. Once he adjusted his expectations for his father according to what was most probable, Daniel found that he became more satisfied with even little gestures on both their parts to reach out to one another. They still fought with each other and argued about politics and sports, but there was no longer any bitterness in their conversations; if anything, it became a playful and affectionate way for them to express feelings without crossing a line that his father might consider unseemly for a man.

Evaluating the Results

This final step represents a transition from this stage of making a decision to act differently to the action plan that follows in Chapter Six. This is where you consider whether you like the results of making a commitment. As Daniel looks back over what he lived through during his own transition from being indecisive to becoming a risk taker, he honestly wishes that there had been some way he could have avoided the pain he endured. Yet now he looks with pride at what he has accomplished. His mentor, his wife, and his father are no longer parts of his life that he thinks of as conflict. Ironically and predictably, they have been replaced by new characters—a sibling who is threatened by his new closeness with their father, a girlfriend who expects things from him that he is unwilling to offer just yet, a competitor at work who has been trying to sabotage his rise up the corporate ladder.

Daniel now realizes that conflict is inevitable in relationships. It is unlikely that there will ever be a time in any of our lives in which we cannot identify at least a few conflicted interactions. These situations do not, however, have to be sources of excruciating anguish, as long as we realize that we do have other options. There is virtually an unlimited supply of alternative strategies with which we can experiment, each of which helps us move beyond blame and toward increased control over the ways we react to conflict.

CHAPTER SIX

Experimenting with Alternative Strategies

IT IS TIME to put what you understand about others, and most importantly about yourself, into action. You recognize the ways that certain people get under your skin, the means by which they attempt to push your buttons. Your unresolved issues from the past are now clearly articulated, or at least not controlling you to the extent that you cannot think clearly or act decisively. Your discomfort has become a helpful ally that has only increased your resolve to act differently in the future. You are willing to accept responsibility for your conflicts, without blaming yourself or anyone else. You are ready to change patterns in your relationships that have become as enduring as any of your most stable characteristics.

There is no longer any sense questioning *whether* you will do something—the only question is exactly *what* will you do? What course of action might you take that is likely to produce outcomes different from those that you have yet experienced? What alternative strategies are at your disposal that will allow you to move beyond blame and into the realm of more constructive interpersonal functioning? How might you react differently, both internally and externally, to the conflicted situations that challenge you the most?

The Alternatives Available to You

"Alternative" means doing something other than what you are doing now. We have already covered a series of action strategies that are part of each previous stage in the process. At this point in the program the emphasis is on helping you break repetitive self-defeating patterns and put into action your resolve and commitment to act differently.

When you are confronted with conflict in relationships, you can choose either (or both) of two courses of action. In the first, you can decide to act differently. This means avoiding the tendency to become defensive or argumentative, to escalate conflicts through your own stubborn determination to "win" a dispute at all costs. The second set of alternatives available to you involves strategies that take place inside of you rather than things you say and do in relating to others. Of course, the course of action most likely to produce significant changes is one that combines the best of both worlds: you not only are able to respond differently on the outside when faced with conflicts, but you also are able to react more constructively internally.

A few words of warning about the suggestions that are to be presented: the use of the word *experimenting* in the title of this chapter was quite intentional. Any new skill or way of relating to yourself or others that you add to your personal repertoire is going to seem awkward at first. You may not feel very comfortable or competent applying the strategies that are discussed. This is only natural. The first time you tried to ride a bike, drive a car, play tennis, ski down a slope, use a computer, or read an intellectually challenging book, it is likely that you struggled quite a bit. You felt frustrated and discouraged. You told yourself that you could not do it, or that it was not worth the effort. If you stuck with it, however, and continued to experiment with alternative strategies until you found the right combination that worked for you, you eventually did reach a point where you appeared fluid and comfortable with what you were doing. The same is true for the tasks that you are about to undertake.

In your efforts to experiment with alternative ways of dealing with conflict, you may not experience much success at first. You may even notice some slight deterioration in the beginning. I mention this not to discourage you but rather to help you be realistic about the magnitude of the task that is before you. You are attempting to do no less than change the lifelong patterns with which you relate to others and yourself; I am not certain there is anything in life that is more difficult. That is why so many people drop out of self-improvement programs and why so many self-help books gather dust on your shelves. When it comes right down to it, changing a significant part of you, especially behavior that is entrenched and enduring, takes tremendous resolve, commitment, and determination. It also takes a willingness to experiment until you can find a strategy, uniquely your own, that works for you.

Make a List and Check It Twice

You will find that the greatest problem is not that there is a scarcity of options available to you in your efforts to alter conflicted relationships; the problem is that there are too many. Imagine, for example, that you are confronted with a situation in which someone is accusing you of doing something that he or she believes was highly inappropriate. You immediately have flashbacks to other times in your life when you were unfairly charged with some transgression. You are thus reacting not only to the present accusation but to the sum total of all such unfair assessments. Fortunately, you realize this.

While ordinarily you might react in a defensive manner, both externally—arguing with the person, trying to convince him or her of the superiority of your position—and internally—desperately trying to place blame elsewhere—this time you decide to apply the process you have learned previously and to experiment with some alternatives.

The method described in this book stresses internal versus external focus of responsibility, integrating the past with the present, acknowledging rather than avoiding pain, and moving beyond blame by concentrating on what is within your power to control. Implicit in this plan is a systematic effort to review internally what you have been doing, noting the typical results and trying something a bit different, some action that is not part of your normal repertoire.

Since you have had a lifetime of practice doing the same things over and over, usually without success, you may have no idea what will work in this situation, but you should have a pretty good idea of what will not work. In your efforts to figure out your best course of action, you first decide to eliminate what you have already tried that has not proven helpful. That way you know what *not* to do anymore, even if you are unclear about what you can do instead.

For example, with regard to the most conflicted relationship in your life right now (or in the recent past), make a list in your head (or better yet, jot notes down on paper) of the characteristic ways that you respond in these situations. Such a catalogue of ineffective strategies for one woman, Elena, looks something like this:

1. *Agree with his assessment and hope this will get him off my case.* "This almost never works since then he interprets that I am a pushover who agrees that he is right and I am wrong. Next time he will just push me harder."
2. *Fight back as hard as I can until he realizes that he can't intimidate me.* "This just makes him even more determined to not back down. One of us may win this particular skirmish, but it will be at the expense of lingering resentments."
3. *Ignore him. Just walk away from the situation.* "He will just bide his time and ambush me later. By then he will have prepared an even more forceful set of arguments to bolster his attacks."
4. *Get somebody else to mediate the dispute between us.* "He would then feel betrayed that I 'tattled' on him by reporting the incident to someone else. He would put on a good show for the sake of the other person's good opinion of him, but he would make me pay later."
5. *Write off the relationship as unsalvageable.* "That has been my most frequent choice in the past when I have been confronted with similar situations. Yet I now realize that the problem is not so much him as it is an interpersonal problem between us. Whenever I have run away from these conflicts before, I have just ended up getting myself in the same mess with someone else."

At this point, you still would not have much of an idea about how to handle such a situation more effectively than you have in the past. You do, however, know what doesn't work. Experience tells you that what you have been doing has not been all that helpful. Rather than repeating those strategies, you might now consider experimenting with something else, *any-thing* other than what you have already been doing.

Some Experimental Alternatives

After working her way through the various steps that have been described in this book thus far—especially concentrating on discovering what specific provocations set her off, understanding how they are reenactments of unresolved issues, and realizing the senseless ways she had been repeating the same mistakes over and over—Elena mobilized her commitment to act differently by resolving to be more experimental, innovative, unpredictable, and creative in her efforts.

Side by side with the unsuccessful strategies she had already tried, Elena created some alternative actions. As is so important in any creative endeavor, she resisted the impulse to censor or criticize herself. No matter how bizarre, radical, or apparently stupid the idea, Elena considered it anyway. She reasoned that she could hardly do any worse than she already was doing. That is the beauty of the freedom you can feel to be more experimental and creative in your responses to conflict. What do you have to lose? What can happen that hasn't occurred already? What do you imagine will happen? That you will fail? So? Better to mess up trying something new, something that conceivably might work, than to continue doing something you already know is fruitless.

Revisiting her list of things she had tried unsuccessfully, Elena jotted down on the next page a collection of alternative courses of action she might try. She was not altogether certain that any of her new ideas would work better than anything she had already tried, but she was fairly optimistic that a few of these options (or a combination thereof) would indeed turn the tables. Following is Elena's list of alternative strategies.

1. *When I look at him, see a clown.* "I've got to stop taking him so seriously. If I could just see the folly in this conflict, I would not react so intensely to the struggle. I will imagine him in a clown suit and try not to laugh."
2. *Imitate him.* "I will mirror everything he does. Whatever he says, I will repeat essentially the same things. If he argues with me, he will just be arguing with himself. That way I won't have to take this so seriously."
3. *Push my buttons before he does.* "Since what gets to me the most is when he starts to bring up stuff from the past (just like my parents used to do), I will introduce my previous mistakes before he can throw them in my face. We can have a contest to see who can remember the most instances."
4. *Order him to do what he is already doing.* "If I tell him to do something that he is going to do anyway, he will either do it (but at least I had some say in the matter) or not do it (and then I will feel more in control)."
5. *Wallow in the pain.* "Maybe I need to feel humiliated, degraded, abused enough so that I just won't take it anymore. Rather than cutting myself off from the discomfort, I can immerse myself in it. That should break something loose."
6. *Ask myself, what are the secondary gains?* "We are both getting something out of this conflict. If not, we would stop. I can recite my list of payoffs like a chant to myself, repeating them over and over until they sink in.

- I like blaming him so I don't have to be responsible.
- I enjoy the passion that comes when the sparks fly between us.
- I need to punish myself for things I have done that I am ashamed of.
- As long as I am focused on our conflict I don't have to deal with other aspects of my life that I am avoiding.
- I get a lot of mileage out of feeling like a victim."

7. *Pretend he's not there.* "I'll just do whatever I want and act like he is invisible. It will be a game I can play. On the outside, I will appear the same to him; on the inside, I will pretend I am alone."

8. *Live with it.* "I can tell myself this really isn't so bad. What is *really* bad is letting this continue and feeling helpless. But this is my choice for now. That's the way it is. I may not like it, but until I am willing to do something else, there is no sense in complaining."

The specifics of Elena's case are less important than the method employed. Once you have attained a degree of clarity and resolve, you will also be able to develop such a list. If the first three, seven, or forty-one things don't work, no problem. There is an endless list of options, limited only by your own imagination and patience.

The Strategy of Managing Conflict

The principles implicit in Elena's list of experimental alternatives are extensions of the method presented in this book. If you wish to extrapolate from this example to your own situation, you will want to consider some of the following guidelines.

1. Be Realistic

Develop a strategy that is within your capability to execute. Michelle, for example, had grandiose plans to teach her boss a lesson, perhaps even get him demoted for his arrogant disregard for employee welfare while pursuing his own goals. She was initially frustrated in her efforts, escalating the conflict to her own detriment, because it was not realistically within her power to make her objective happen. She adjusted her goal to a more modest wish to stop allowing her supervisor to abuse her. This narrower objective was well within her means to achieve.

2. Stay Focused on Your Objectives

Don't let yourself become distracted by things that are not important. Clearly define what it is that you want, and then go after it.

Dan has a competitor at work who has been trying to undermine him in hopes that he will be passed over for promotion. Every time Dan has allowed his attention to be drawn away from his ultimate goals and has engaged his adversary in direct confrontation, they both have ended up looking foolish and unprofessional. By measuring each subsequent action in terms of its likelihood of increasing or decreasing his probability of promotion, Dan has been able to thoughtfully ignore, parry or retaliate against any initiative without losing sight of his objective.

3. Do the Unexpected

Never underestimate the value of surprise. When you are predictable, you may easily be defeated. This is true on any battlefield.

129

Marilyn felt stymied in her attempts to get her mother to stop meddling in her life. She tried pleading, to no avail. Threats, punitive responses, and ignoring her were equally ineffective. Like so many people locked into dysfunctional cycles of conflict, Marilyn kept trying the same things over and over.

Applying the strategy used by Elena in the example mentioned earlier in this chapter, Marilyn also decided to be unpredictable in her responses. Instead of resisting her mother's suggestions, she experimented with compliance. Instead of arguing, she decided to agree with everything her mother said.

Although this particular tactic did not work any better than others she had tried, Marilyn learned from this encounter that even when she tries something new that does not work, at least she is not repeating the same useless strategies that she *knows* are ineffective. She now feels more free to try a number of creative ways to deal with her mother in the future. Even though her mother continues to meddle, Marilyn feels less perturbed by the circumstances since she *gave herself* more options for how to respond.

4. *Take What You Can Get*

Rather than lamenting about what you are not able to accomplish, concentrate instead on what is within the realm of possibility.

Patrick had been negotiating with his son for some time, trying to get him to agree to some equitable arrangement such that if he dropped out of college for a year, then he would have to support himself during the interim. Their relationship, which previously had been quite good, had deteriorated to the point where they could barely speak to one another in a civil manner.

It could well be conceived that this was a necessary conflict between them, one that would launch the young man into the world as a more independent and self-sufficient person. For the present, however, Patrick just wanted a way out of his predicament without compromising the important principle of accepting responsibility for one's decisions.

During one point in their heated discussions, the son altered his position. He seemed most adamant about controlling his own destiny but less concerned with the specifics of any contract between his father and him.

"You mean as long as you can take next semester off with no interference from me, you are willing to abide by terms we would agree on?," Patrick asked tentatively.

Once they reached that breakthrough, Patrick was able to build into their contract the resolution of a number of other disputed issues that his son was readily willing to settle. Although both of them ended up getting what they wanted, Patrick felt especially good about making progress on a number of fronts during that critical moment of opportunity.

5. Create as Many Options for Yourself as You Can

By choosing a strategy that permits you the flexibility of moving in several different directions, toward different objectives that are equally desirable, you ensure that you will get at least some of the concessions you want.

Kara felt taken advantage of by her sister Krystal after the death of their father. Still struggling with her own grief, she was also saddled with all of the responsibility for taking care of their invalid mother, making funeral arrangements, and settling the estate. The only thing that Krystal seemed to care about was the amount of her inheritance.

Kara discovered that by trying to do everything herself, she was falling behind in her own personal and professional responsibilities. It was clear she had to have some help, but she had yet to find a way to recruit Krystal's assistance in even the most minimal way.

Applying the tactic of multiple options, Kara was able to tether a number of tasks to monetary compensation by the estate. Whether Krystal helped as executrix, nurse, or financial manager now seemed less important since Kara would receive payment for her efforts. Once she began her new ploy, sure enough Krystal wanted to become involved in the chores as a way to usurp her sister. Kara hid her delight with the obligatory protest, eventually succumbing to pressure that she allow Krystal to help out.

6. Don't Argue with Someone Who Is Looking for a Fight

In other words, there is no sense in launching an initiative when another person is ready, willing, and able to repel it.

The fence that separates Myron from his neighbor is more psychological than an actual physical barrier. Unfortunately, Myron and his neighbor have been feuding for years, and Myron has been on the losing end of their exchanges. This is not only because the neighbor is the one with the dogs who bark all night but also because he does not appear to be the least bit perturbed by their conflict. On the contrary, he seems to savor the war.

The most serious mistake Myron made was to escalate their feud to the point where the neighbor engaged in deliberate acts of annoyance rather than just negligence. Myron became terribly predictable in his responses—yelling across the fence to show his displeasure or squirting the dogs with a hose. In both cases, the neighbor filed a police report for harassment.

Partly out of exasperation because he could think of nothing else to do, Myron allowed things to cool down. Even though his sleep continued to be disturbed by the barking dogs, he turned on a noise suppressor and ignored the disturbance as best he could.

Within this relatively calm climate, he visited other neighbors who were within earshot of the dogs and organized them into a posse to approach his adversary. With this coalition showing a firm alliance, the neighbor agreed to take steps to curb the problem.

Each of these principles applies to experimental *interpersonal* strategies that break the chains of your usual way of functioning in conflict situations. Although most conflicts involve parties who are sincerely interested in resolving their differences, these concepts will serve you well with opponents who may refuse to negotiate and are only interested in domination.

Some Things You Can Do Internally

In an earlier section I asked you to imagine a situation in which you have been unfairly accused of doing something that caused a major conflict. No matter how you have tried to rectify the situation, you feel impotent and misunderstood. You have created a list of things you have tried and are quite amazed at the sheer number and variety of strategies you have employed. You notice, however, that most of them have involved interpersonal methods in which you have tried to alter someone else's behavior. Such approaches generally don't work.

In reviewing his list and checking it twice, Arthur determined that it did not seem to matter very much what he said or did with his brother; they would still end up in a serious misunderstanding. He tried being compliant, being assertive, showing first more trust and then more power—whatever he tried ended in the same result. It was clear to Arthur that the solution to this problem would not come through any negotiation with his brother. The key for him was to give himself whatever comfort he could internally so that he would no longer be so disturbed by their interactions.

Since Arthur was unwilling to cut off all communication with his brother (in spite of their conflicts, he still loved him), he had to discover a way that he could spend time with him without suffering indignities. He experimented with a number of internal strategies until he found the right combination.

1. Redefine What You Are Experiencing

It was Arthur's interpretation of his brother's behavior that led him to conclude that he was being humiliated, taken advantage of, or ridiculed. Since he could not change the way his brother acted toward him, he decided to alter his perception of that experience. This task was made considerably easier by the insights he had developed into the source of their unremitting tension—their competition as children and what each represented to the other. These realizations made it easier for him to be more forgiving of what his brother was doing and why. This did not mean that he was excusing his brother's conduct—just that he now understood what was behind it. There was no longer any reason for him to assign blame.

Arthur decided to redefine what was taking place between them as a normal form of sibling rivalry. Whether that was an accurate interpretation of the situation was beside the point. Such a reconception allowed him to not take the conflict so personally, as if this were something being done *to* him. Instead, he found it much more helpful to think about what was happening as similar to their wrestling matches when they were young. Conflict was the way they related to one another, in much the same way that some people show affection by nagging or arguing with each other. Arthur certainly did not like the texture and tone of their relationship and the limited, hostile ways they dealt with each other, but before he could possibly do anything about that he first had to center himself such that he was not unduly disturbed by their encounters.

Much to his surprise, redefining their struggles as a form of brotherly rivalry helped Arthur refrain from overreaching in subsequent interactions. Sure enough, this change in his attitude de-escalated the tension between the brothers to the point where they settled into a less emotionally charged style of communication. Of course, his brother attributed this change to Arthur being less stubborn. Rather than igniting a new argument about who was at fault, Arthur showed considerable restraint and graciousness by not taking up the challenge and instead expressing that whatever was the cause of the changes, he was grateful that they could now enjoy each other's company. The key to this change in external interpersonal response was lodged in the internal strategy to redefine the problem.

2. Purge It and Let It Go

Tell somebody—a friend, a partner, a therapist—what is bothering you and then drop the subject. When you cannot reason with someone, when you are not able to change the pattern of your conflicted interactions, then at least minimize the effects of the struggle.

Imagine yourself doing this right now. Picture yourself unloading all your pent-up feelings, your indignation and frustration, toward a particular person. I am certain this is not a new experience; you may have already spent a considerable amount of time doing just that—telling select others about the ways you feel you have been mistreated by someone. This time, however, after you have expressed all the emotional intensity inside you, imagine these feelings draining away. Let them flow out of you so that you feel your load lightened. Resolve to stop torturing yourself by reliving the conflicts over and over.

There are two ways that you experience misery as an effect of conflict. The first involves the hurtful things people say and do. Second, and just as potentially lethal, is what you say and do to yourself before, during, and after the encounter. If you are unduly hard on yourself and self-critical, if you are obsessed with blame and guilt, if you replay over and over in your mind all the injustices you have suffered, then you are hurting yourself as surely as if you had cut yourself with a knife.

A conflict can occur once in your life, or you can live it over and over again a thousand times. You can drive yourself to distraction by nursing your resentments, rubbing salt in the wounds, savoring the victim role in which you have placed yourself. You can keep yourself up all night by playing back arguments, browbeating yourself for not saying all the things you wish you had said. You can distract yourself all day as well, reliving the worst scenarios you have experienced. This goes well beyond trying to learn from the encounter, trying to figure out what you could do differently next time. Through such self-inflicted misery you punish yourself for what you believe was a less than stellar performance. You make yourself pay for losing your cool or acting spinelessly. Now that you have invited somebody to move into your head, you are allowing him or her to live there rent free.

You take this critical person into your bed at night. You invite him or her to join you on the ride to work. You take him or her into the shower. Wherever you go, whatever you are doing, the conflict remains alive in your indignation.

You cannot do a single thing about what has already happened, but you can decide how much you want to let the incident control you now. How long do you want to suffer? How much do you want to stew over the matter? When you have decided that you have had enough, what can you do to let the negative feelings go? Who can you talk to? What do you need to do in order to stop torturing yourself by reliving the conflict over and over?

Under the right circumstances, catharsis does work. Tell somebody what is bothering you. Dump your troubles out on the floor. Let go of whatever happened. Put the past behind you.

3. Rehearse Through Imagery

Much as you did in the previous chapter, in which you imagined the conflict situation you fear the most, try to visualize yourself in the predicament. Note how you appear—your body language (placating or rigid or fierce). Hear how you sound—your voice tone, pitch, and modulation. See how you handle the situation.

Now, in your mind, alter this image of yourself in such a way that you appear calm, in control, no longer distracted by unresolved issues from the past. You are now utterly composed, fluent and convincing in your point of view, yet no longer threatened or made defensive by what the other person is saying or doing. Quietly, dispassionately, you attend to what is going on, noting what seems to be working and what is not. Without a vested interest in a particular strategy, you find you are able to change direction in midair just like a basketball player outmaneuvering an opponent with sleight of hand, a head fake, or a forceful dunk. (Create your own metaphor if you are not a basketball fan.)

When the exchange is over, even without a resolution and with continued animosity, observe how you are able to shrug it off readily. Get inside your head and listen to how this image of a more fully functioning you processes the experience. There is no blame directed toward you or the other person, no remorse or guilt, no second guessing about what you should have done. Instead there is a deliberate processing of the experience and then a resolve to try some different things next time. Finally, watch yourself put the whole incident aside and move on to something else, with few lingering side effects.

4. Become More Reflective

Writing in a journal is an ideal way in which to help yourself make sense of your behavior, analyze recurrent themes and patterns, experiment with new ways to process your experiences. When you spend structured time involved in self-analytical endeavors, you become more reflective about what you do, why you did it, and what you could do instead.

This book began as a journal writing activity for me, trying to figure out why I have had trouble with the same kinds of people in similar positions throughout my life. Perhaps, like you, I am sick of wasting my time and energy feeling consumed by the aftereffects of conflict. Writing down my thoughts and feelings and recording the dialogues that have taken place help me keep things in perspective. Since I have been keeping a journal since I was seventeen I have the added luxury of being able to review patterns throughout my life. I noticed the same issues cropping up again and again—my craving for approval from older men, my competitive drive to overcome core feelings of inadequacy, my vulnerability to being hurt because I am too trusting—these are but a few of the recurring themes. By writing about them and subsequently reviewing what I was experiencing, I am better positioned to avoid repeating the same mistakes.

Writing in a journal affords you the opportunity to problem solve, to recollect ideas you want to access, and to rehearse what you want to say both to yourself and to others. Sometimes this helps you let the feelings go so you don't have to tell the other person, who may not be receptive to hearing you; at other times you are able to prepare more carefully for what you want to do and how you want to do it.

5. Stop Taking This Stuff So Seriously

It may feel to you as if your conflicts are life-and-death struggles, but in the grand scheme of things, one hundred years from now who will remember or care about whatever you are struggling with in your life right now?

Humor serves us well by introducing some balanced perspective into the picture. For example, in a gathering of associates two colleagues continuously went for each other's throats, creating tension and morbidity among the whole group. It took the intervention of a third party to break this pattern: he parodied what was going on in such an accurate and hilarious way that even the combatants broke into grins. This diffusion of negative energy takes place when you are able to laugh at yourself and your tendency to greatly exaggerate the significance of minor skirmishes.

The methods suggested here involve internal strategies to help you cope with conflict situations. Yet there is only so much you can do within yourself, especially considering the interactive nature of conflict. The insights you have developed, the patterns you have attempted to understand and work through, have value when they can help you *act* differently in your style of communication.

Experimenting with Ways to Counteract the Forceful Demands of Others

The process we have been working with is likely to be difficult to apply, concentrating as it does on what you do internally to counteract blame, in situations in which you must deal with forceful or manipulative individuals. Despite your attempts to identify your own buttons that are being pushed, work through conflicts from the past, commit yourself to act differently, follow through on a specific plan, you still may encounter some resistance from others. This section explores strategies for situations in which people are determined to get their way at your expense and you must resort to more creative efforts to counteract their attempts.

Dealing with Unreasonable Demands

There are times when people ask you to do things that they well know are beyond what you are willing to do. They ask anyway, as a test of your commitment or loyalty or to prove their potency in enlisting compliance to their demands.

"I don't mean to intrude like this, but I was wondering if you could help me. You said that you would do most anything, and I know this is a lot to ask, but . . . "

Say no and you will face an escalating series of more forceful strategies to gain your cooperation. Say yes and you will temporarily appease this person's appetite, but at the expense of your own needs. You will feel resentful or abused—that is, if your self-esteem is high enough for you to realize you deserve to be treated differently. If this is not the case, you will swallow your indignation and do what is demanded, hoping you will not be bothered again for a while. But, of course, you will because you just taught this person that although you may not like it and you will make some noise about it, if a person works on you long enough you will accede to their demands. Your reluctance makes the victory even more enjoyable for people who manipulate others in this way. Not only do they get what they originally asked for, but they also have the satisfaction of knowing they got you to do something that you did not want to do. Imagine how powerful that must feel to such people.

In such instances, and in the presence of the other styles of manipulation discussed here, it is important to follow the dictum of professionals who work with these types of people for a living: *In response to unreasonable demands, set reasonable limits—and stick with them no matter what.*

Defusing the Threat of Self-destructive Acts

Some people are willing to go to almost any length to exert an illusion of control. Pain and suffering do not have the same meaning for them that they do for others, or they may have a tolerance for misery that is beyond mortal thresholds.

"If you won't let me go to the game, I will just end up staying at home doing nothing. I won't get any work done under these circumstances, when you have aggravated me so much already."

This is not an idle threat. We know that some people are willing to forgo things they really want in favor of the greater pleasure of manipulating someone else into getting upset. Children will flunk exams, quit jobs, stay home from the prom just to demonstrate that they will not be controlled. Spouses will walk away from marriages just to prove that they will not give in. Businesses suffer financial losses because workers deliberately lower their productivity in order to punish their employers.

Threatening to do something to hurt oneself is actually quite an effective manipulative strategy. Two friends agreed to pool their efforts in an attempt to obtain tickets to a playoff game. Because of their cooperation and division of labor they were successful in their goal, but there the goodwill ended. A conflict developed over who got tickets to which game. Rather than working through the stalemate to the satisfaction of both people, admittedly a time-consuming and frustrating struggle, one of the friends threatened that he would just sell the tickets, or better yet give them away, and neither of them would go. To prove he was serious, he stopped the next passerby and asked her if she wanted some tickets to the playoffs—cheap.

Manipulative people continue to engage in manipulative behavior because it works for them. There is nothing more fearsome than an army that is prepared to fight without the possibility of survival just to keep others from reaching their goals. Most of us not only want to win, but we want to come out of the interaction better off than we were before we started. Since people who threaten to hurt themselves just to get to you do not operate by fair rules, there is no way to win in an exchange with them—they will shoot at you, and if that does not work they will shoot themselves in the foot and blame you for the wound.

The best way to get somebody to stop doing something is to make it less fun or profitable for them to continue. Since the manipulative ploy is based on eliciting a particular reaction in another, it is important that these people not be allowed to enjoy the benefits they think they have earned. Essentially this means not challenging threats directly, but defusing them dispassionately.

Applying this technique to the child who threatens to sabotage his schoolwork if he is not allowed to go to a game, the parents would respond as follows:

"Gee, that would be unfortunate if you allowed your aggravation and disappointment to get the best of you. And we would certainly be sorry to see your schoolwork suffer as a result. We respect your decision to handle this matter the way you think is best. Of course, if your grades do suffer, we will assume you are telling us that you need help. Maybe a tutor could be scheduled every Saturday night until you feel you have things more under control."

Saying No to Guilt

It is a hallmark of the seasoned manipulator to keep trying different strategies until one is found that really works. A little girl who first threatened to eat a caterpillar if her mother did not buy her a book she wanted tried another tack: "Oh, it's all right, Mom. I know we need to spend our money on really important things like purses and stuff." She got the book.

Guilt works best between children and parents—in either

direction. This is because in both roles there is a lingering feeling that we could and should have done more for the other person. My son does not finish his chores in the yard. I casually but conspicuously head outside to complete the work. He is watching television and does not even notice. I come in for something I forgot, and finally he realizes what I am up to. "Oh, Dad, I'll take care of that," he says, and rises to help. "No, it's okay," I reply stoically. "I'll take care of it since you are too busy." He is a quick study and not at all shy about turning the tables. "Dad, would you like to play catch with me since you're hardly ever home on the weekends with all the traveling you have been doing lately?"

It is a funny thing about guilt that even when one is aware of what the other person is doing, there is enough truth embedded in the accusation to stoke up support for the request. All the while we feel resentful of the attempt to manipulate us, we still go along with the program, baffled as to how it all happened.

Somebody who is very good at influencing people to do things they are reluctant to do has a highly developed sensitivity to vulnerability in others. I know this because that is essentially what therapists do—guide (and sometimes cajole) people into doing things they believe are good for them. Guilt preys on all the unfinished business of your life, wherever you still feel the need to rectify past mistakes.

To immunize yourself against attempts by others to "guilt" you into doing things you do not want to do, you must first accept your own fallibility. Dinah knows she is not a perfect mother. Her chief struggle during the past decade of her life has been coming to terms with some of the misguided decisions she has made regarding her daughters. If she could do things over again, there are a hundred ways she would act differently—chiefly, she would be more consistent, and she would listen more to what her daughters have to say.

It is acknowledged between mother and daughters that serious mistakes were made. Dinah apologized to her daughters as the first step in what she believed would lead to forgiveness and adult friendships. Instead, this admission provided the daughters with leverage to insert a dagger and twist whenever they wanted money or a favor.

The manipulation stopped only after Dinah was able to accept fully her own imperfections. So she made some mistakes. Had she known then what she knows now, she would have done things differently. But she did the best she could with what she knew at the time. She can accept that now. If her daughters cannot, that is their problem. She will no longer be emotionally blackmailed into buying their support.

A Few Reminders

There are many unscrupulous individuals in the world who are willing to resort to any measure of deceit in order to sell their wares, promote their ideas, or recruit followers. They rise to the top of their fields because they are willing to do more than anyone else to get what they want. Lying? Cheating? Stealing? Deceiving? No problem. The end justifies the means. The end they are looking for is one in which they are on top and everyone else is on the bottom.

What is one to do with someone who is obsessed with power and control? *Stay out of his or her way.* When that is not possible (as often it is not), when you are not in a position to extricate yourself from the relationship and avoid future conflicts, follow these rules.

145

1. Remind yourself that it is not intelligent to trust that this person will do as he or she says.
2. Do not set yourself up for betrayal. Since the manipulative person is predictable in attempts to be manipulative (by definition), do not be surprised or indignant when it inevitably happens. Plan accordingly.
3. Refuse to be baited. Once you realize what is happening, take a step back so that you do not escalate the conflict.
4. Talk to yourself in such a way that you stop blaming the other person for doing what he or she does best. Stop blaming yourself for mistakes you have made in the past. You can't do anything about the choices you have already made or the actions you have already taken.

Some people do not operate under the same rules as you and are willing to resort to tactics that you find offensive. This does not necessarily make them bad or wrong or demented. Moving beyond blame means no longer focusing on the other person's behavior. It involves taking inventory of your options, letting go of things in the past that are no longer within your control, and teaching other people how to treat you differently. Perhaps, as discussed in Chapter Seven, in time you will even come to see conflict as potentially useful in teaching you things you could never learn any other way.

The Positive Functions of Conflict

YOU ARE FUMING with indignation. Earlier in the day you spent the better part of an hour arguing with someone who absolutely insists that he is right and you are wrong. You, of course, are equally convinced that he is the one who is misinformed and misguided. Furthermore, you have devoted several more hours to reliving the experience, reviewing exactly what was said and how thoroughly you were misunderstood. The more you think about the matter, the more upset you become.

You feel awful about the way your interaction proceeded. You have some minor regrets about the manner in which you conducted yourself, but most of your disgust and disappointment is directed toward your adversary: he had no right to speak to you that way, nor was he very fair in the style with which he dealt with you. Now that you think about the matter further, you are convinced that there was little you could have done to circumvent this struggle. Yet you feel angry, frustrated, and completely at a loss as to where things went wrong.

Given the intensity of your lingering emotions, the gut-wrenching anguish you feel that makes you want to scream out in rage, what possible value could there be in such an exchange? What good is conflict if it only leads to mutual antagonism?

147

From the preceding discussions throughout this book you might easily get the impression that conflict is a bad thing, a situation to be not only dreaded but avoided at all costs. While I am not suggesting that you go looking for arguments or that you should rejoice when you find one, I would like to point out that conflict can have some important positive functions. There is a big difference between chronic, destructive conflict, about which you feel you can do nothing, and productive conflicts that serve some greater purpose.

The familiar encounter I just described does not *only* lead to greater frustration and animosity. These types of experiences also encourage us to reflect on our conduct, as well as on the behavior of others. Conflict is an intense, intimate kind of engagement between people. It signifies that you and another person both feel quite strongly about your positions. More than that, it means that you are both willing to risk fighting for what you believe by exposing yourselves, intellectually and emotionally.

Conflicts can help you test out your most cherished ideas by bouncing them off others who feel equally strongly about their perceptions. It is through disagreement with others that you are most easily able to determine what it is that you care about the most. These dialogues might not be very pretty to listen to; they certainly are not pleasant to experience. They are, however, instrumental in promoting growth and stimulation, reducing tension, and getting you what you want.

Before we move on to applications of the book's process to specific situations in love (Chapter Eight) and at work (Chapter Nine), let us take a look at the positive side of conflict. Once you learn to conceive of it as a relatively normal, predictable, even helpful part of human relationships, you will find it much

easier to respond to conflict situations as temporary pro
to be solved rather than as crises that will destroy your life.

When Conflict Helps

Most often, conflict is viewed as a breakdown in communication, a failure to relate to one another in a civilized, constructive manner. The term has become associated with such concepts as *hostility, provocative action, war,* and *impasse.* It is certainly
true that certain types of conflict—most notably those in which
weapons and/or physical or verbal abuse are employed—are indeed destructive enterprises that leave casualties in their wake.

Yet without conflict, without disagreements of any kind,
imagine how boring, predictable, and conventional your life
would be. If you were to get everyone to agree with you all of
the time, no one would ever challenge your thinking and actions. You alone would be responsible for all decisions without
having your reasoning examined.

You may have often wondered why people do not get along
better, why we often resort to such forceful, disagreeable ways
to impose our will on others. Why can't we just avoid conflict
altogether and instead use negotiation to arrange compromises
between opposing points of view? Even if this were possible,
it might not be desirable. When people abide by fair rules of
engagement, demonstrate a degree of flexibility, and show a
reasonable concern for finding solutions rather than simply en-
joying a good fight, conflict can be highly useful and instructive as a means to advance the development of individuals, as
well as that of our society.

For example, conflict with skeptics forces scientists to test
and retest their ideas and make more cogent and convincing

arguments in favor of change. Social psychologists Dean Pruitt and Jeffrey Rubin have made the interesting observation that three of the most influential thinkers of the past century have all viewed conflict as not only helpful but crucial for human survival. Charles Darwin's theory of evolution is based on the notion that intraspecies struggle leads to survival of the fittest, whose genes then strengthen the stock of future generations. Sigmund Freud based his theory of the human mind on intra-psychic conflict between instincts and conscience; a whole generation of developmental psychologists then followed his lead and created models explaining human growth in terms of progressive stages that are driven by internal conflict. And Karl Marx created a sociopolitical philosophy based on the idea that inevitable conflict between human agendas moves us to a higher level of functioning.

All three of these conflict theorists recognized that progress and evolution do not come without some cost—whether in the form of inconvenience, discomfort, pain, or even fatalities. Change is not a pretty sight, even if we do enjoy the end result. The most magnificent building was engulfed in scaffolding and covered with construction scars during its transformation. Any work of art can appear singularly unappealing until it is finished. Even a beautiful baby was just a blob of cells before it completed its growth. Similarly, conflict may be viewed as an ugly event, a period of temporary instability, before consensus is reached and change takes place.

The Constructive Functions of Conflict

In addition to its role in facilitating change, conflict serves a number of other constructive functions—as a releaser of tension, a promoter of growth, a regulator of distance between people, a path to intimacy and to personal gain, and a preventer of stagnation. The intention here is not to convince you to go looking for opportunities to argue at every turn, but rather to help you realize that what makes fighting so intolerable is the belief that it serves no useful purpose. It is extremely important when you find yourself embroiled in controversy to ask yourself what functions the conflict is serving.

- How is this disagreement helping me focus my attention on issues that I have been neglecting?
- What cues leading up to this eruption did I miss that signaled impending escalation of feelings?
- What can I learn from this encounter that will be helpful to me the next time I am in a similar predicament?
- What is this conflict doing for me, however annoying its side effects, that I might accomplish in other ways?
- What are the underlying issues that we are both really upset about?

When you can articulate even a few of the functions that conflict may be serving in your life, you will find it much easier to stop blaming yourself and others for the predicament. On some level, you can feel grateful for the path you are headed down, even if the journey is uncomfortable. This is not unlike the feeling you have when you undertake any adventure: things are unpredictable, frightening, stressful, uncomfortable, and exciting— all at once. You want the journey to end: if only you could be back home where it is warm and safe! Yet you also revel in the exhilaration of facing the unknown. Look to these functions of conflict as reminders that this process is really an adventure.

Conflict as a Releaser of Tension

What determines whether conflict is likely to lead to constructive gains or dangerous escalation are the intentions of the parties involved. If the implicit goal is aggression, coercion, or the submission of others, ultimately somebody is going to end up worse than before he or she started.

When all parties are working toward mutually satisfying goals, when they demonstrate flexibility in their methods of problem solving, and, most of all, when they show respect for one another, conflicts can help air grievances, resolve resentments and frustration, and release tension. Children, for example, learn at a very early age the values of conflict in building coalitions and social structures. The games they learn to play (marbles, Monopoly, fantasy) and the activities they engage in (athletics, coloring at tables, group work) are designed to teach them the skills of settling disputes constructively. They learn how to let off steam in socially appropriate ways. Rather than lashing out in frustration, throwing tantrums, or subverting others' goals, children learn through these games how to negotiate for what they want. This behavior is an integral part of the social responsibilities and roles in which we must function as adults.

Katrina and Marna, two sisters who live together, have developed ways to let off steam when one sister becomes frustrated with the other's annoying behavior.

"Marna drives me crazy," Katrina explains, "especially when she leaves dishes in the sink when she could so easily just put them in the dishwasher. I think she does it on purpose just to aggravate me."

Marna quickly retorts, "I do *not* do it on purpose, and don't tell me that leaving dishes in the sink is any worse than your disgusting habit of not flushing the toilet at night."

"I am just trying to be considerate and not wake you up during the night. Every time *you* flush it always disturbs me."

They are now off and running, bickering about the behaviors that bother them. Yet when pressed on the matter, both Katrina and Marna acknowledge that their conflicts over little things seem to prevent them from fighting over other, more explosive issues that might jeopardize their relationship and their living arrangement. As with so many people who live together, controlled conflicts act as safety valves in which normal frustrations and tension may be expressed safely.

Conflict as a Promoter of Growth

A number of developmental psychologists have pointed out that most human growth occurs as the result of conflict. Disputes with others challenge us to reflect on our beliefs, eventually moving beyond our current cognitive capacities to more sophisticated methods of reasoning. Unless you experience conflicts and challenges, there is very little likelihood that you will be motivated to search for higher-level ways to solve problems. For instance, if I were to challenge your political beliefs in such a way that you began to question the validity of some of your assumptions, you would then have to search for a more complex, highly evolved set of beliefs that more accurately reflect reality.

Conflict may be helpful not only in facilitating your personal growth but also in promoting improvements in your relationships. Learning to resolve disputes effectively is a major life skill that we should have learned as early as preschool. Even at an early age, children have the capacity to master myriad

153

social skills useful in resolving conflicts—social sensitivity, problem solving, communication methods, ways to get needs met without alienating others in the process.

I recall one representative incident from teaching preschool. Nickie, a rambunctious four-year-old boy, grabbed a truck away from Jennifer in the sandbox and then threw sand in her face. Jennifer promptly took a truck (fortunately rubber) and plunked Nickie on the head with it. He then burst into tears and ran to me for help. I escorted Nickie back to the battleground and instructed Jennifer and him to settle the matter between themselves without resorting to violence.

My attention was momentarily diverted by another child who refused to come out from under a picnic table. By the time I returned to the scene of the dispute Nickie and Jennifer were in the throes of serious negotiations not unlike those of politicians, attorneys, or diplomats.

"I'll let you have my cookie during snack if I can have my truck back," Jennifer suggested as her first offer.

"You don't even like those cookies," Nickie responded. "Besides, it's not *your* truck," he was quick to point out.

The whole interaction did not last more than two minutes, but I was stunned by their degree of sophistication in applying some fairly complex negotiating skills. They ended up playing with the truck together. Since they had never been friends before this conflicted exchange, I could only conclude that their disagreement helped each of them grow a bit in their interpersonal skills.

Conflict as a Regulator of Distance Between People

Certain relationships, especially those between family members, tend to become enmeshed. The boundaries between spouses, or between parents and children, become so fused that it is difficult to determine where one person ends and the other begins. They become like the sea slug and jellyfish of the Bay of Naples that attach themselves to one another so that they may both survive; each needs the other's contribution in order to digest food. During this process, biologist Lewis Thomas muses, each individual organism loses its sense of self—the two become one being.

This metaphor of two fused selves has some interesting implications for relationships that, in contemporary vernacular, are described as "codependent." Such connections, originally designed to offer protection, mutate to the point where one person cannot function independently without the other suffering as a result. The child cannot separate from his parents. One spouse cannot go anywhere or do anything without the other in tow. Two friends use each other as crutches that, at the same time they provide support, also keep them crippled. When one of them attempts to assert some independence and socialize with someone else, the other will sabotage that relationship using guilt or manipulation: "I haven't been feeling very well lately. I called you for help last night, but I guess you were out with what's-his-name." The distance between them subsequently closes to previous levels of dependency. The boundaries between them fuse together, each identity subsumed by the other.

A similar phenomenon occurs with parents and children. When the child attempts to assert herself, to establish her own life, the parent(s) may be unable to let her go. They need the child "triangulated" between them in order to keep their own relationship stable. When she was away at college, they fought more often. At the prospect of her graduating and moving out on her own, they are moving toward divorce. But if they could only keep her around . . .

155

Novelist Len Deighton once remarked that if children and parents did not fight, they would never leave home. Then the world would end. Conflict acts as a distancer between people who are overly close and need to create space between themselves—for both their sakes. As a case in point, two co-workers began their jobs at the same time. Lonely and overwhelmed, they gravitated toward one another for mutual support. They ate their lunches at the same table, confided their frustrations to each other, and hung out together at every opportunity. While initially this support was invaluable, their relationship became a liability, insulating them from networking with others. They both knew they needed to let go and expand their connections, but they were reluctant to do so. It felt like letting go of a life preserver in the midst of a stormy ocean.

It took a conflict, albeit a manufactured one, to drive a wedge between them that would motivate more independent action. They found a reason to take opposite sides on a department policy debate that became pretty ferocious. After this public disagreement, it became clear that they were not clones; it was as if they searching for a way to highlight their individual differences so that they could assert more independence. They were able to remain friendly, but the closeness between them was reduced considerably, to the benefit of both. The conflict acted as an impetus to adjust the distance between them to a more functional level so that they could expand their base of friends.

Conflict also maintains stability in relationships by permitting people to express themselves when close proximity and prolonged contact inevitably spark friction and irritation. The alternatives to conflict are avoidance and withdrawal, solutions that initially prevent clashes but ultimately lead to irreconcilable differences.

Conflict as a Path to Intimacy

Good communication does not take place only when two people are calmly, rationally, and politely taking turns presenting their points of view. Granted, this is the time when people are most likely to hear one another, as well as respond sensitively to what is being said. Most assuredly, this type of relating promotes greater closeness and intimacy between friends, lovers, co-workers, and parents and their children. But it is not the only way this outcome may be achieved.

The things we feel most passionately about, the ideas we hold most dear, are not necessarily those we can convey in the most controlled manner. For example, I know that I will stay perfectly calm in a conversation only if we stick to safe, relatively superficial subjects in whose outcomes I feel I have little at stake. If, however, you really want to *know* me, in the deepest sense of that word, if you want to know my innermost thoughts and feelings, my manner will not remain calm and dispassionate. In order to get closer to me, you must risk contact that is potentially more explosive. By getting into the realm of basic values and beliefs, by sharing our most honest reactions and feelings, we both risk driving each other away as much as coming closer together.

Conflict is a kind of passionate, committed communication in which both people are expressing points of view that are important to them. When the interaction is carried through to its successful conclusion, conflict can become a turning point in creating a new level of intimacy in a relationship.

Two adult brothers had maintained a cordial but distant relationship ever since they both left home. They sent cards to one another on appropriate holidays, called on each other's birth-

157

days, visited during annual family reunions. There existed an uneasy, carefully controlled truce between them, not unlike many male friendships in which the content is limited to safe, superficial areas—their jobs, sports, reports on their respective achievements. These men had hardly ever had a disagreement between them because they were both so careful to stay away from any subject that was possibly controversial.

Inevitably, during one routine phone conversation one of the brothers mentioned an opinion that was unusually personal, to which the other brother responded in kind. Before either was aware of what was happening, they were screaming at one another for the first time since they were children. Their carefully negotiated agreement not to be personal with one another quickly evaporated. They both slammed down the phone and vowed never to speak again.

Yet this conflict opened a crack that needed to be addressed if they were ever to have an intimate relationship. Once they were able to calm down and resume their discussion at a heated but not intolerable level, they found they could talk about a number of subjects they had always wanted to broach. It was not unusual at this new level of intimacy for one or both of them to feel upset. Sometimes they would break off for a while in anger. But once they both had a taste for how much more satisfying a deeper relationship could be, conflict became the path for them to become more intimate.

Conflict and Winning Valuable Gains

There are things you want that you could never have without conflict. Some battles are worth fighting, especially when what you hope to gain outweighs what you might lose if you were to avoid the skirmish. You are thus inclined to risk escalating a conflict by aggravating someone when you feel that the issue is important enough to press your point of view. There are times when the potential prize is so valuable, or the potential loss of something is so crippling, that you may even be willing to go to war. In fact, only a few societies have ever been discovered that do not seek to shed the blood of their neighbors in their efforts to fight for a principle or territory that is considered dear to heart.

Biologists, anthropologists, and other scientists have demonstrated that human beings are endowed with certain aggressive propensities that help us survive in a hostile world. Throughout human history, the tiniest of insults or slights perceived by one monarch or another has led to retribution on a scale that kills millions.

Lest we resort to blaming our genes or human nature for our inclination to engage in conflict, it is also important to realize that many instinctual responses that once served us well but are now obsolete have been brought under control. Whereas it is true that the vast majority of cultures do engage in regular warfare, there are some peoples that eschew all violence, such as the !Kung San of Botswana and the Semai of Malaysia.

Even if our biological instincts have programmed us to be aggressive, through our will and cognitive capacities we can channel that energy toward creative pursuits. It is thus entirely possible that conflict can help us win gains we consider important without having to resort to aggression.

Earlier in this book I described the case of Nat, a young man who continually got into brawls with people he believed had offended him. This is a risky, expensive method to resolve conflict, one with serious consequences for both parties. Nat eventually learned that he could be just as persuasive and effective battling for principles he considered important without resorting to physical violence. This more "civilized" method does not, of course, prevent adversaries from operating under a different set of rules, but that is something that you cannot control.

The important point to remember is that in order to get something you really consider valuable, you are likely going to have to work for it. Conflict with others, who also covet the prize, is the price you pay.

Conflict as a Preventer of Stagnation

Throughout human history new discoveries; innovations in thought; and creative contributions to literature, science, and art have often met with resistance. Being branded as a heretic for spouting radical ideas, imprisonment for introducing novel concepts, exile, burning at the stake, crucifixion, ridicule, and humiliation by one's peers—these are the fates that the Galileos, the Freuds, the Walter Raleighs, the Joans of Arc, the movers and shakers of our society have met.

Ideas that conflict with the status quo make us feel uneasy; they undermine our notions of reality. Take, for instance, this rule enforced by our parents when we were young: don't swim after you eat because you will get stomach cramps, and then you will suffer a hideous death curled up on the bottom of the pool. I recall many hot summer days spent sitting on the edge of the pool, dangling my feet in the water, watching the other kids, waiting for my lunch to digest.

"Hey, Ma, when can I go in the water?"

"What did you eat for lunch?" she would ask with the skill of an interrogator who could see through any attempt to lie.

"Just a hamburger and french fries. But I didn't eat my pickles."

"An hour," she would say with the assurance of an actuary who had all the data at her fingertips. And then I would sit impatiently watching the clock, trying to negotiate for an early release.

Many years later I sat in a scuba diving class listening to the instructor's last-minute instructions before our first open water dive.

"Now remember," he continued, "be sure to eat a big breakfast before the dive or you will get hypothermia from the cold water."

"Ah, excuse me," I quickly inserted, "but won't we get stomach cramps and die if we eat before we go in the water?"

He must have seen the panic in my face, the flash of all those hot summer days I had spent waiting on the edge of the pool, for he very gently pointed out that that myth had been debunked years earlier. Why hadn't anyone told my mother, I wondered.

The point is that even if someone had told her, I doubt she would have paid any attention. I could have argued with my mother all I wanted, brought in a team of experts to substantiate my claims, and I doubt it would have done any good. We just don't give up dearly held ideas very easily. It takes conflict to challenge our assumptions and stimulate a change in our beliefs. Arguing with others and defending our cherished principles are what drive us to develop them further, or abandon them in favor of others that have a closer approximation to reality.

Conflicts can take a number of forms beyond what we ordinarily think of as arguments.

Conflicts in human relationships are inevitable. In many ways, they are even necessary if we are ever to advance our knowledge and live with each other's differences. There is no sense in blaming ourselves, or anyone else, for getting us into arguments or disagreements; that is the logical consequence of taking a stand on issues that are important to us, of not compromising our standards in the face of pressure. In Chapter Eight we look more closely at the value that conflict has in our lives as individuals and as members of an evolving society. Nowhere is this value more evident than in our most intimate relationships.

CHAPTER EIGHT

Conflicts in Love

THE METHOD DESCRIBED in this book for moving beyond blame and resolving conflicts, especially through internal processes, can be applied to the relationships with which you struggle the most—those close to home and heart. The more you care for somebody, the more energy you probably have committed to that relationship. Whether with spouse or lover, parent or child, sibling or friend, when one of these relationships is not going well, you are truly having a bad day. Or month.

These are people who really know you. They know how to get to you when they so choose. They are invested in getting you to do things that affect them directly. You cannot easily let go of them or write them off. You are bound to them by biological ties, vows of commitment, or strong feelings.

Michael and Gary have been friends since they were kids. Once upon a time they had much in common—they played games together, hung out with the same crowd, shared similar goals and interests. As adults, however, each man developed in quite different directions—vocationally, socially, and especially in terms of basic values. This, of course, is not surprising when you consider the changes each person undergoes on a daily or weekly basis, much less over several decades. That is one reason it is difficult not only for friends to remain close over a period of many years, but also for spouses. Conflicts are inevitable between spouses and between friends like Michael and Gary, because individuals grow and change at different rates and in different directions.

Michael and Gary are linked together more by their past experiences than by their present compatibility. When they are not talking about the good old days, they are usually arguing— about where to meet for lunch, about who will pick up the check, about whose life is more fulfilling, about anything and everything. The truth is that Michael does not care very much for the time he spends with his old friend: he is tired of their arguments. Yet something stops him from walking away from the relationship. Call it habit. Call it obligation. Or call it love. He does feel deeply for Gary even though their time together is often tense and unpleasant.

What Is Different About Love Relationships?

Before Michael can begin to understand what his conflicts with Gary are all about, before he can identify the underlying issues and work to change the way he responds internally and externally to his friend's provocations, there are some things that he must understand are unique and different about love relationships.

Failure to See Reality

Any disagreement between two people represents a conflict of interests, a clash of goals. In conflicts with those you love, your feelings tend to cloud your judgment. You make excuses for those you love that you would never make for others. Someone at work might forget to do something for you, and you write him or her off in a minute. If someone you love does the same thing, you may make allowances for his or her behavior. This tolerance for neglect may lead to situations in which you begin to see a loved one not as he or she really is, but (a) as you prefer to see him or her, or (b) as you remember him or her to be.

Any attempt to resolve a conflicted relationship must take into account the distortions that are likely embedded in your perceptions of one another. In order to understand clearly why you are in conflict, the origins of the disagreement, and what you might do to change dysfunctional patterns, you first will have to do a careful "reality check" to make certain that you are responding to what is really happening rather than to your fantasy.

Enmeshment

Love involves a connection to another that implies commitment, intense feelings, and mutual dependence. While the term *codependent* has gotten a bad name through overuse in recent years, this may simply mean that two people who care about one another have come to hold certain expectations, not an unreasonable state of affairs.

When dependence becomes pathological or destructive, two people in a love relationship have fused to the point where they stop functioning as independent beings. *Enmeshment* is the term that best describes what happens when people, especially family members, become overinvolved in each other's lives. Conflict develops whenever a person seeks to express individuality or autonomy.

165

Love relationships present additional challenges in the con-flict arena since you have to determine how your disagreements are serving to maintain the status quo of mutual dependency. Michael notices, for example, that his friend Gary is most in-clined to start a fight just after he has related a story of how independent he has become in recent years. Gary feels left out, mourns the loss of their prior closeness, and takes perverse plea-sure in experiencing intense engagement with Michael by pick-ing a fight. At least Michael cares enough to argue with him, he reasons.

Emotional Intensity

Love is, by definition, a strong feeling of caring. It is the name applied to that emotion of concern, that bond that holds two people together. It would only make sense that the more you care for someone, the more potentially explosive a conflict could become. Sometimes, if you could only care a little less, you would not react in such extreme ways with such little provocation.

A friend or co-worker asks me to do something. I politely decline, pleading other commitments. My son asks for a ride to school. I also tell him that I have other things to do; he will have to walk or ride his bike. This time, however, we have the makings of a fine argument, perhaps even the possibility of a full-fledged conflict that could last well into the evening. Why do the most ordinary of disagreements sometimes turn into such out-of-control conflicts with the people we love? The an-swer is found in the intensity of our feelings for one another.

The more you care for someone, the more deeply you are committed to one another, the greater is the potential for ex-plosive outbursts that can escalate into major conflicts. Any attempt to resolve disputes with loved ones must take into consideration the higher level of emotional intensity, which can make it more difficult to identify the patterns behind whatever is going on.

Furthermore, there may be a long history between you, one that creates lifelong bonds inextricably tying you together. This can complicate matters considerably because it is difficult to be sure exactly what you are really fighting about.

Underlying Conflicts

A key element in resolving disputes is to figure out what you are really in conflict about. Just as there are unresolved issues from your personal past that affect the ways you respond to conflict in the present, so too are there underlying interactive issues that are part of every relationship's history.

Sometimes we fight over things that do not really matter because it is safer than getting into an argument about issues that are more risky and emotionally charged. A wife, for example, picks a fight with her husband over his habit of leaving his dirty clothes heaped over a chair, spilling onto the floor, rather than picking them up. He retaliates by attacking her for her lack of support during this busy season in his life.

What they are conveniently avoiding is the real issue they are both upset about: they have not had sex in over three weeks. Each time one of them attempts to initiate lovemaking, the other is too tired to respond. They are reluctant to talk about their sex life, which both feel has become routine and boring; they are afraid their lack of physical intimacy may escalate into an even greater conflict between them. So they argue about safer, more mundane matters, which may not lead to resolution of their underlying conflicts, but at least they do not rock the boat.

One other way that core issues between people become buried or displaced into other, less threatening interactions is in symbolic form. Certain communications become a metaphor for the real conflict that lies beneath the surface. In the dialogue below, what do you think the couple is really in conflict about?

HE: Have you looked at the plans for the new house?

SHE: Not really. I just glanced at them.

HE: So what do you think?

SHE: They're okay. But I don't like the idea of a stucco facade. I would much rather have brick—it's sturdier.

HE: Look, we've gone over this again and again. If we use brick we won't have enough money to decorate the interior the way we want.

SHE: So who cares about furniture and wallpaper if the damn house isn't solid in the first place!

HE: Don't yell at *me*! What good does it do to spend all our money using more expensive materials if we have to sit on the floor?

SHE: You are exaggerating. I don't care if we just stay where we are. Why do we have to move at all?

HE: Fine! Let's just forget the whole thing!

If we start with the assumption that what this couple is fighting about is a metaphor for their core conflict, we can look beneath the surface to decode their basic struggle. Their fight over the construction of their house is a symbolic representation of their disagreements over life-style. Throughout their married life appearances have been most important to him while solid (but sometimes unattractive) foundations have been her priority. He cares most about the daily details of their life together—which restaurant they go to for dinner, which couples they socialize with, how they dress when they go out— while she is most concerned with the quality of intimacy they feel for one another. She would just as soon stay home as go out, as long as they are taking care of one another and the foundation of their relationship.

Each wants a home befitting his or her respective self-image. If this couple were to engage in dialogue about their real conflict, rather than its symbolic form, the conversation would go something like the following.

SHE: I want a simpler life, one in which we forgo luxuries in order to have more free time to do what we want.

HE: I *am* doing what I want. And I like having money to buy nice things.

SHE: I would rather that we use the money we have to save for more security in the future.

HE: Who knows if we will be alive to spend it in the future?

We have here a dispute over basic values, not a fight over a house. Until this couple begins to recognize what they are in conflict about, until they think differently about their struggles, they have little chance of resolving their differences. Without a change in the direction and style of their exchanges the conflicts between them are likely to escalate out of control.

You will confront a similar challenge in attempting to move beyond blame and resolve conflicts with a loved one. Before you can expect to settle a dispute with anyone, especially with someone with whom you are intimately involved, you will have to figure out the underlying issues that you are really disturbed about. Unless you can do so, a minor disagreement may spin into a conflict out of control.

How Conflicts Get Out of Control

In examining the mechanisms of how fights escalate, family dynamics experts have noted several common elements. These elements can aggravate matters that are already sensitive and feelings that are already raw.

1. Heaping Issues on Top of One Another

Adding more and more tension to an already stressful situation, family members bring in material from the past in order to marshal support for a weak argument.

"This is just like what you've done before. Remember the time you said you had taken care of the reservations but you really had forgotten? And another thing that has been bothering me . . . "

2. Personal Attacks

Combatants stop dealing with issues and start attacking each other personally. No longer are they content to win a fight based on the merits of their perspectives; now they want to smear each other's character and destroy completely any credibility the other might have. The conflict has now moved beyond a dispassionate debate about a particular problem into the realm of humiliating someone as a human being.

"It figures you'd say something like that. A person of your gutter morality and incompetence has no choice but to resort to such tactics. I'm not surprised in the least by this, and *neither is anyone else*."

3. Adding Weight to an Argument by Bringing in Others

The last phrase in the preceding example, thrown in almost as an afterthought, escalates the personal threat of an attack by bringing in the alleged support of others to fortify one's position. When someone says to you "everyone knows what a louse you really are" or "just the other day I heard people saying the same thing about you," the person is trying to add weight to an otherwise groundless accusation. It works, too, as you are likely to respond even more defensively.

4. Other Factors

There are also several other factors that can cause conflicts to spin out of control:

- When issues move from shades of gray to absolutes of black and white
- When people expect the worst from others and then make their prophecies come true by treating them as if they are despicable
- When motives shift from attempting to settle a disagreement to trying to defeat an opponent
- When people are trapped (or trap themselves) in an untenable position
- When people are fighting over things that don't really matter in order to avoid issues that are really important

In each of these cases, trust between the individuals is breached. They have become suspicious of one another's motives. They seek to control the exchange as a first priority rather than concentrating on trying to reach a mutually satisfying agreement. They are no longer concerned with resolving their differences—only with saving face in others' eyes and placing blame elsewhere. Under such circumstances, one or both participants will resort to one of two postures, withdrawal or aggression; both are counterproductive.

Preemptive Intervention During Withdrawal and Aggression

The object of conflict intervention is to change the patterns of interaction *before* things get out of control. This means being able to recognize the first signs and symptoms of imminent crisis *as they are occurring*. Depending on whether you observe a person withdrawing or engaging in aggressive high gear, you will want to act swiftly to change (1) the climate of the exchange, (2) the balance of power, (3) the style of interaction, and (4) the potential for loss of face.

Let's examine both possible scenarios and look at how they would be handled differently. In the first case, you sense the person is starting to close down and withdraw; in the second instance, you observe the beginnings of escalation.

Case #1: Withdrawal

Initially, both Fred and his stepmother, Natalie, seemed equally vested in planning a surprise party for their father/husband. Since this was a relatively late second marriage for Natalie, there was an uneasiness between Fred and her based on his perception that she was a newcomer and thus not really part of the family. When Fred attempted to take over the planning, Natalie stepped in to assert her role as the primary decision maker.

Although she was pleased when Fred began deferring to her

rather than arguing so vehemently about minor matters, as he had been doing a short while ago, she sensed that this change did not bode well for their future relationship. Fred might give in on the planning of the party, but it would be at the expense of increased resentment and future escalation of tension between them.

How did Natalie notice this change taking place? She monitored closely throughout the exchange not only her own progress toward the stated agenda but also Fred's reactions and responses. She observed the following symptoms:

1. A change in Fred's demeanor (passivity, acquiescence, complacency)
2. A change in the climate (from heated debate to disengagement)
3. A change in style (perfunctory agreement without challenges)
4. A change in content (from the controversial but important issues to those that are more safe and superficial)
5. A change in communication (from equal interaction to one-sided exchanges)

Notice in the dialogue between them how obvious these signs are.

NATALIE: So what do you think about inviting his friends from college?
FRED: (Shrugs) Sounds fine.
NATALIE: So you think that's a good idea?
FRED: (Impatiently) Sure. Yeah. Whatever you want.

Natalie will need to intervene if she wants to bring the interaction back to a level of congruent engagement without reaching the previous destructive levels. She can accomplish this in several ways.

Immediacy. "I sense that you have given up talking to me. I feel sad about that because I very much value your input."

Labeling what you see. "I notice that you have become more passive, as if you no longer care what we decide."

Parallel matching. Adjust your behavior in terms of intensity and level of engagement to that of the other person. When Fred becomes quiet, Natalie tones herself down rather than picking up the slack. This gives him the chance to reengage.

Exploring underlying issues. "I don't think we are really arguing about the party. We both care for your father and we seem to be competing for his approval. Let's talk about what is really bothering us."

Capitulation. "I seem to be doing most of the talking. How about if I back off for a while and you decide the rest of these things?"

Each of these interventions signals that Natalie has noticed the change that has taken place, recognizes this is a crucial juncture in her relationship with Fred, and has elected to do something to change the pattern and style of interaction rather than allow things to deteriorate further. She has chosen to take some risks rather than be complacent, to confront problems rather than avoid action because of fear of making a mistake. You will find that other people will give you a lot of latitude in your efforts to be helpful when they sense you are only trying to work things out.

Case #2: Aggression

Discussions between brothers James and Jonathan about where they would vacation together had been proceeding quite well. James wanted to head for the beach, Jonathan for the ski slopes. They were at the point where Jonathan was about to give in (withdraw) when he abruptly changed direction and started blaming James for manipulating him. James helplessly watched things between them turn ugly as Jonathan became more aggressive and belligerent. Specifically, the following signs were in evidence:

1. Abandoning issues for personal attacks ("You always do this to me.")
2. Using threats to influence the outcome ("Forget it. I won't go.")
3. Increased hostility ("You are such an asshole!")
4. Escalation of the argument ("Since we can't agree on this, maybe we should just not go!")
5. Movement away from issues toward pointless arguments ("Besides, I just got new skis and now I can't use them.")

As in the first case, if you do not intervene to change the direction in which the conflict is headed, serious damage is possible. In this example, however, efforts are made to deescalate the aggression and blaming rather than initiate direct confrontation:

Reflection of feelings. "I can see that you are really upset about the way things are going."

Limit setting. "If you would lower your voice and calm down a bit, then we could talk this through."

175

Apology. "I am sorry for pushing you. I hope you will forgive me so that we might resume the discussion."

Redirection. "We seem to have gotten off track. Let's back up and start again."

Self-disclosure. "I am also upset with the way this is going. I love you, and I am sorry that we are treating each other this way."

In any situation in which one person has escalated the conflict, it is clear that the stakes for that person are high. The person who is more in control needs to intervene in such a way that any loss of face is restored so that negotiations may begin again. The one time when efforts to resolve disputes are likely to fail is when aggression has escalated to the point where actual verbal or physical abuse is in evidence.

When Family Disputes Get Out of Control

Studies have shown that an individual is more likely to be harmed by a relative than by anyone else. This applies not only to physical forms of abuse but also to emotional cruelty.

Interestingly, abusing our family members is a relatively recent phenomenon among our kind. In the days before doors were invented, when we lived in caves or open spaces, it was impossible to inflict harm on a child or spouse without everyone else in the tribe knowing about it. Once privacy was "invented" through demarcated living quarters, it became possible for people to do things without being closely monitored.

With the advent of privacy, it has become possible for people to take out their frustrations on and act out violent conflicts with those they purport to love the most. These are the most passionate of disagreements, the ones that are the most chronic and the most destructive and that elicit the greatest sense of helplessness. They are the conflicts that most often mask hidden motives, buried resentments, and unresolved issues from the past.

As the following phone conversation between a daughter and her mother illustrates, each participant feels helpless to change the way they interact. Their struggle is a repetition of the basic conflict they have been living out since the daughter first demanded, when she was still in the crib, that the mother choose between her and her father as the most important person in the house. By refusing to set limits or establish appropriate boundaries, the mother has "taught" her daughter to abuse her.

MOTHER: Dear, can I get you anything when I am shopping today?

DAUGHTER: Why are you always bothering me? Don't you know I'm busy this time of day? [*She just drives me crazy with her offers to help.*]

MOTHER: I'm sorry, honey, I was just trying to help. [*I guess I should have known better.*]

DAUGHTER: Damn it, mother! Being sorry doesn't help. You interrupted my train of thought. What did you want anyway? [*I hate being so rude to her, but I can't help it.*]

MOTHER: Nothing important. I just wanted to hear your voice. [*She is so busy and now I've aggravated her. I don't blame her for being mad.*]

DAUGHTER: Look, Mother, you just can be such a pest. Why don't you get a life or something, and

177

leave mine alone? You're always meddling. [*If I don't keep her in line, she will really get out of hand telling me what to do.*]

MOTHER: I don't mean to. I just wanted to say hello. [*If I make her any more angry, then she will never let me see her.*]

This is just another in a series of abusive conversations in which each participant makes excuses for inflicting or tolerating pain. Blame is directed either outward or inward, but in both cases negative feelings grow to the point where resolving the conflict is much more difficult than it ordinarily would be.

Combating Abusive Behavior

The bottom line is that abusive behavior is a *very* effective way for someone to get what he or she wants. So what is the incentive for such a person to change? The abuse will not stop until it is no longer tolerated.

Confront Your Own Denial

Once you accept the reality that someone in your life is treating you in disrespectful, abusive ways, you will feel increasingly uneasy about what you are experiencing. This is the stage I discussed earlier as intensifying your discomfort: in order to be motivated to change, you will first have to feel uncomfortable, if not downright miserable, with the status quo.

The function that denial serves, as a defense mechanism, is to protect you from an onslaught that your mind feels would be too much for you to handle. Unfortunately, the side effect of this process is that it permits you to continue suffering in silence, partially anesthetized to the pain you are suffering.

When you are ready to dismiss denial as an ally, you must be prepared to deal with all the discomfort it has been protecting you from facing.

"It took a friend who approached me to get my attention. After one especially vehement attack, he whispered to me, in astonishment, how could I take that? I asked him what he was talking about. I hardly noticed. I had become so used to the yelling and ranting and raving, I thought it was normal. Then I started to feel even worse."

The feelings of anger and resentment that are being blocked by denial of the abuse are what will motivate you to take a stand against further disrespect.

Respond to Violations of Your Rights

It is difficult to change the rules of any relationship in midstream. Imagine sending out a memo that reads: "I have decided to no longer permit you to treat me the way you have been. The next time you speak to me in a raised tone of voice, threaten me, or otherwise act inappropriately, I intend to do the following. . . . "

It is one thing to resolve to do things differently and quite another to be taken seriously. Just because you express to those who are treating you poorly that you do not like the way things are going does not mean they will alter their styles. In some cases they may even laugh at you and redouble their attempts at domination.

You therefore must be prepared not only to declare your intentions but to follow through with them. Whereas in later chapters you will be exposed to a number of specific ways to combat abusive or manipulative behavior, it is important at this point to realize that you must do *something* even if you do not know what that might be. One thing for sure, you know what *not* to do, and that is to endure abuse as if it is all you are entitled to.

Whatever strategy you select, whether a form of direct confrontation or indirect control, you will need to remind yourself constantly that you deserve better. You are entitled to reasonable treatment, and you will never get what you want unless you go after it.

Knowing Your Needs and Expressing Them

You have two kinds of needs—those you know about and those you do not. If you are unaware of what you really want from someone, and are thus unable to articulate what it is that you wish, how is it possible for you to ever feel satisfied in that relationship?

It would certainly be nice if people could read our minds and know what it is we are looking for even before we know ourselves. What a delightful surprise it would be to have those desires satisfied before we even had to ask. But in reality, except in unusual circumstances between lovers who are communicating on a similar plane, such expectations are ludicrous.

A husband asks his wife how her day went, but what he really wants is for her to tell him how much she missed him. She answers his question. He feels rejected and pouts. She ignores him. An argument is about to begin.

One brother tells another that he is skiing beautifully. He has never seen him ski quite so well. "Thanks," he mutters sheepishly and then points to the beautiful scenery around them. The first brother had been fishing for a compliment about his own skiing and now feels hurt. At the first opportunity he snaps at his brother, who is now feeling hurt as well.

180

A woman asks a friend for an opinion about a recent decision she made. Taking her at face value, the friend offers input that opposes the decision. Actually feeling quite insecure, the woman had been looking for support rather than an opinion. Now she feels put down and belittled even though she got exactly what she asked for.

This is the kindling that starts the flames of conflict. You feel demeaned, misunderstood, neglected, perhaps even taken advantage of by someone who has no idea what you wanted in the first place. It is one thing to feel angry at someone who knowingly withheld something you wanted; it is quite another to be disappointed because that person could not anticipate your needs before even you were aware they existed.

That is why it is so important that you take responsibility for identifying your own underlying needs and desires, and then making certain they are clearly stated so they can be fully acknowledged and understood. I know this sounds good, but it is quite another thing to put this commitment into action.

The first step is for you to know what your needs are. Perhaps a better word to use might be *desire* or even *preference* or *want* since *need* implies that it is something you require in order to survive. Although life might feel empty or unpleasant without certain elements such as reassurance from peers, a primary love relationship, or civil interaction with one's parents, these are not actually necessary in order for you to live. Except for food, water, shelter, and a few other basics, everything you want is a desire rather than a need.

With that distinction in mind, what are some of your wants and desires that have remained hidden or unexpressed? This is hardly a choose-from-a-list question since the possibilities are endless. Nevertheless, perhaps a few of the following items will trigger your own dormant desires that you have been reluctant or unable to ask for in your relationships:

- I want to be told that I am valuable, cherished, that my presence is important.
- I wish to feel that it is safe to ask you for something and have you say no; I wish it to be equally safe to say no to you.
- I want to be spoken to in a calm manner that demonstrates respect for me and for what I have to say.
- I want to know that I have made an impact on you, that you have heard, understood, and responded to what I offered.
- I prefer that you initiate things with me as often as I do with you.
- I would like shared responsibility for decisions that are made rather than either one of us shouldering an unfair burden.
- I want you to check out how I am feeling and care enough about the answer to respond appropriately.
- I want to know that it is safe to make a mistake with you and that I will be forgiven.
- I would like you to reach out to me when you sense that it is hard for me to express what it is that I want.

This last item on the list is the great equalizer. How lovely it is when someone is sensitive enough to be able to read what you might be wanting, and to be willing to check out that perception. I would not count on this as a usual state of affairs, but it is not unreasonable to wish that we all could attend closely enough to each other that we could, on occasion, help people state more clearly what it is they really want.

I'll Scratch Your Back. Will You Scratch Mine?

It is difficult for people embroiled in conflict to talk to each other in a civilized way when most of their recent interactions have been tainted. They are on guard, defensive, and mistrustful. One of the most common, and sometimes most unhelpful, strategies of my profession is to invite people to come into therapy sessions and talk about what is wrong. If all you think and talk about are negative facets of a relationship, if all you do is complain about the injustices being done to you, you will continue to feel steeped in bile and blackness.

One delightful alternative, quite effective with conflicted couples although certainly applicable to any love relationship, is to focus on positive, loving things that you can do for one another. They might include initiating more hugs, calling one another on the phone, giving one another undivided attention for a predetermined period of time, expressing feelings of affection. The object of these tasks is to balance the anguish of conflict with other aspects of a love relationship that are more nurturing and supportive.

While this strategy may appear quite simple and effective, it only works when both people are willing to set aside the conflict temporarily in order to work on a more positive style of interaction. Unfortunately, because some people *like* the power and control associated with conflict, it is not always easy to put these commitments into practice. As we shall see in Chapter Nine, this is as true for problems in relationships at work as it is for those at home.

Conflicts at Work

IF YOUR PRIMARY conflicted relationship is not with someone you love, the next most likely possibility is that it involves someone at work. Perhaps even more than any other setting, the workplace is a territory that is partitioned according to one's position, degree of authority, connections, and power. Conflict is an intrinsic part of individual struggles to determine one's own agenda, to advance oneself above and beyond others, and to maintain control.

Customizing Strategies to Settings and Situations

The program for countering conflict described in this book involves the systematic process of identifying underlying issues, understanding their origins, and taking responsibility for changing both the style of interaction and your reactions to what transpires. Implicit in this method is the realization that you are likely to experience considerable discomfort during the journey toward resolution and that you will have to take some risks in order to experiment with alternative strategies.

However useful this procedure might be, it is still a "generic" program that must be customized to fit your particular needs.

What might work for one person will not be appropriate for another. What will prove helpful in one setting or situation may very well backfire in another. What will turn out to be effective with loved ones may not be at all successful with those at work. It will be up to you, therefore, to adapt what has been described in a way that increases the likelihood that your efforts will be rewarded.

For example, one of the distinguishing characteristics of the workplace is the prevalence of a rigid hierarchy of power. Conflicts frequently arise because one or more persons feel that their positions or territory are being threatened. You will most often find yourself in disagreement with co-workers because either they are attempting to exercise control over you or they perceive that you are trying to do so with them. Given this particular climate in which you must deal with such conditions of power and control in conflict situations, you will wish to make some adjustments in the ways you approach skirmishes at work.

1. Identifying What Sets You Off

You will recall that this first stage in the process is where you begin by determining what it is that you are feeling, thinking, and doing that you find so upsetting. In the work setting, these will most often center around feelings that (a) you are not being appreciated, (b) you are being undermined, (c) someone is attempting to control you, or (d) you are in a win-lose situation in which there is a good possibility that you will not end up victorious. Essentially, all of these areas center around threats to your security and sense of competence in what you do for a living.

Identifying what is at stake, and where and how you are

allowing yourself to be set off by the conflict, gives you the edge you will need to regain control of yourself even if you have no control over the other person. Dana, for example, works as an elementary school teacher. One of the more senior members of the staff has taken it upon herself to enforce what she believes are professional standards that everyone should live up to. Dana feels tremendous resentment toward this woman, whom she neither likes nor respects, for attempting to control her.

Recognizing what most consistently sets her off (attempts to control her professional independence, threats to her freedom of movement, attacks on her personal integrity), Dana is in a much better position to react to her colleague in a thoughtful, calm manner than she might be otherwise. Although she has yet to figure out how to deal with this person (it is still early in the process), she has already found some ways to reduce the intensity of her own reactions.

2. Exploring the Origins and Causes

Most of us spend more of our waking moments at work than we do in any other setting. Given this prolonged exposure to people during the very stressful circumstances that usually accompany work, it is highly likely that our unresolved issues are going to play themselves out in this setting in particular. Any needs for affirmation and reassurance? Fears of failure? Sense of futility? Any unresolved issues with authority figures? Any ongoing sibling rivalries? These and a dozen other themes in your life come alive every day during your interactions with others at work.

Dana searches for the source of her extreme reactions to

her colleague's attempts to control her. Big deal that she thinks she knows what is best for her and everyone else. Why can't she just ignore the lady and go on about her work?

For one thing, Dana realizes that the hierarchy of power in her school is such that she does not feel safe challenging this woman. Dana does not have the power base she would need in order to assert herself. She feels like an orphan, stranded on her own to fend for herself. It is no coincidence, of course, that Dana was adopted as an infant. However irrational her fears growing up, she could not help but wonder what would have happened if she had been a "bad girl." Would her parents have taken her back to wherever they found her?

Dana became a teacher primarily because she wanted the freedom of not being part of an oppressive system. Prior to this career she had worked in an insurance agency and had felt smothered by how accountable she was to her bosses and co-workers. Finally she has her own classroom, and yet she still feels helplessly controlled by others. Of course, like so many conflicts, this circumstance is more a matter of her perception than the actual state of affairs. In reality, the other teacher has no more power over Dana than does anyone else in the school. The key to this problem is that Dana *feels* controlled, not that she *is being* controlled.

3. *Allowing Yourself the Discomfort*

Although feeling uncomfortable with your self-defeating behavior does lead to change, you will probably not wish to show these feelings of vulnerability to others. It is often not safe to telegraph any feelings other than complete confidence and competence at work; otherwise, you may be judged in ways that may jeopardize future opportunities.

There is, naturally, the exception with confidantes whom you trust completely. Dana did feel that there was one person at school with whom she could talk openly. When she unloaded her frustrations to this friend, she did feel better. She remembered, however, that the goal of her efforts was not to *feel* better but to *act* better. Over the weekends, in particular, when she could not confide in her friend, she noticed her anger and frustration growing. While at first these resentments and blame were directed toward her controlling colleague, eventually they began to turn inward: she started to feel depressed and helpless over the way she was allowing herself to be intimidated.

4. Taking Responsibility Without Blaming

In response to all the manipulation, control, and game playing that go on at work, there is a greater than usual tendency to blame others for acting in ways that you believe are unfair, insensitive, or inappropriate. Because what you do is so interconnected to the assigned roles of co-workers, there is usually a lot of blame to spread around, if that is your intention.

It thus takes even greater self-control at work to resist the temptation to blame others for your problems. There is always somebody around who you believe is not doing his job the way you think he should. Your supervisor could always show more appreciation and consideration for your efforts. The administration could always be more responsive to your needs. The economic climate could always be better.

Dana tried all these excuses and more. Why wasn't her principal showing her more support? Why weren't others in the school standing up to this control freak? Why did she get stuck with a classroom in such close proximity to this lady? It was all so unfair.

189

Dana accepted that which was not within her power to change. She could not alter the past, nor could she help the fact that she had been an orphan and had struggled most of her life with feeling alone. Dana could not make this woman act any differently just because she did not like her the way she was. She also could not avoid run-ins with this teacher for the time being; there was no way she could pretend that the problem would go away.

There were, however, several things that Dana could control. She did not have to let this woman get under her skin. It was *her choice* to react so dramatically to behavior that, actually, was only a bit annoying. In fact, she noticed this woman did not treat her any differently from anyone else. She observed several other colleagues ignoring this woman completely. Others simply shrugged off her comments as a mild inconvenience. Clearly it was possible for her, too, to change the ways she reacted to this woman such that major conflicts would be reduced to minor disagreements.

5. *Committing Yourself to Act Differently*

This is the one stage that is considerably easier to implement at work than at home. Because co-workers are less involved in your life, more compartmentalized, less emotionally connected, it is easier to make changes in the patterns of interaction. Heck, all day long, memos are sent out announcing changes in policy or in the ways business will be conducted. Change is such an integral component of work settings that it is considered business as usual for an employee to announce intentions to do things differently.

Dana was surprised at how easy it was to tell first her friend,

and then later others, of her intention to no longer be so concerned with what others had to say about her style of classroom
management (with the exception of her principal). She declared
at lunch one day, in front of a fairly large group, that she had
been paying too much attention to what others thought instead
of trusting herself more to develop her own style. She spoke
euphemistically about her resolve to ignore her colleague's attempts to control her.

It was not as if this mere commitment to act differently
solved the matter of the conflict with her co-worker. If anything, the woman took this announcement as a challenge to
redouble her efforts. This public statement, however, acted as
an impetus for Dana to follow through on her plan to no longer
allow her unresolved issues to control her present behavior. She
finally realized that it was not this woman who was her nemesis: it was her own past.

6. Experimenting with Alternative Strategies

This stage takes a bit of adjustment as well. There are things
you might try in attempting to resolve conflicts with family members that you would never try with co-workers. Customizing
the change program to work settings means using methods that
are consistent with what is expected in that environment.

For instance, direct confrontation was unusual among this
group of elementary school teachers; inviting someone to lunch
to discuss a matter in indirect terms was more the norm. Many
of the "power tactics" to be discussed in the next section may
be useful in corporate or other settings, but they would have
minimal use in this particular school.

Going through her list of options, Dana decided to try "applying a little sugar" in her interactions with her colleague. Instead of making snappy, cynical retorts, or arguing with the woman directly, she tried an opposite tack: every time an attempt was made to control her, Dana thanked the woman for her concern. Whenever the woman tried to meddle in her affairs, Dana calmly backed down from challenging her directly.

I might add that this strategy did not work any better than anything else Dana had tried previously. As I mentioned earlier, the particular method employed is less important than the determination to keep experimenting until something works. What changed in this example was the way in which Dana processed her experience of conflict internally. She no longer blamed this woman for making her life miserable. Just as important, she did not blame herself for being so acquiescent. Instead, she concentrated on doing the best job she could in her classroom, building a support system of like-minded colleagues, and insulating herself as much as possible from the power struggles that had previously zapped her energy.

Power Tactics

It is impossible to talk about conflict at work without addressing issues of power. Whether dealing with social revolutions, racial or ethnic strife, ideological debates, geopolitical disputes, or interpersonal conflicts, power is at the core of attempts to achieve objectives in the face of competing interests. Each party seeks control of the situation, often at the expense of the other's position. Disputes between states, as well as individual disputes among friends, family, or co-workers, typically involve struggles over possession of limited resources (oil, money, territory, power). In Dana's situation mentioned earlier, her colleague was using intimidation as a way to control that which she coveted most—power within the school hierarchy.

As with Dana's situation, the intent on the part of some people in work situations is to intimidate you into submission. This can be accomplished through explosive anger or, more often, through subtle or indirect means.

Withdrawal. *If you don't do what I want, or follow where I wish to lead you, I will detach myself from you. I won't respond to you in any of the ways that matter most. Did you say something? I don't care. I have nothing to say. You no longer exist as far as I am concerned. Once you comply with what I want, then I will become responsive again.*

Criticizing. *I will blame you for everything that is going wrong. It is all your fault. If only you were more intelligent/perceptive/sensitive/competent/experienced/strong (choose one), then we wouldn't be in this situation. I will ridicule you, make jokes at your expense, keep you on the defensive so you remain helpless and under my control. Because I am so much better at being critical than you are, you had better not put up too much of a fight, or then I will really turn up the heat.*

Overpowering. *I will overwhelm you with my anger to the point where I appear dangerous and out of control. Be careful not to push my buttons since I can't be held accountable for what I might do. If you attempt to challenge me, then I will really become frightening. I could do anything. You should just wait until my rage has run its course. We will both feel better that way.*

Undermining. *I will discourage you through indirect methods of sabotage. I will abuse you behind your back, never to your face. I will bad-mouth you to others, all the while pretending to be helpful. I will forget things I don't wish to remember. I will put you down in subtle ways so you cannot be sure what I really meant. If you confront me directly, I will act hurt, as if you are the one abusing me.*

Discounting. *I will ignore you in such a way that you feel like dirt, not even worthy of my attention. I will demean whatever you say, negate everything you do. By my actions, it will be clear to you that I don't think you matter. If you attempt to address this issue with me, I will respond haughtily as if I have no idea what you are talking about. I will twist things you say and interpret things you do in the worst possible light. I will frustrate you to the point where you will do or say something you regret. Then you will look really stupid.*

There are a number of other power tactics that co-workers or supervisors use in conflict situations to influence their result. Once you are able to recognize these common patterns of manipulation, you will be much more able to take a step back from the victim/blaming position and instead offer a counterresponse that defuses the power tactics employed. For each of several manipulative strategies that are used to exert power I have included examples of how you might parry them.

Postponement

Move: "I would prefer to talk about this later."
Countermove: "I hear that is what *you* would prefer. I would rather we deal with this right now."

Refusal to Acknowledge Conflict

Move: "I don't think we have a disagreement at all."

Countermove: "I am glad you feel fine about this. Since I still have some lingering doubts, I would like you to indulge me and continue the discussion."

Pre-cuing

Move: "I can't believe you even brought it up."

Countermove: "I can see this is uncomfortable for you. Ignoring the problem, however, will not make it go away."

Gunnysacking

Move: "It is not just this one incident. You also . . . "

Countermove: "Wait a minute. Let's take these issues one at a time. Otherwise we are going to end up bringing up stuff that we can't deal with."

Fogging

Move: "You have made a legitimate point with that first thing. Let's deal with that."

Countermove: "I agree it might be better to deal with the issues one at a time. However, several of them are related, and the first point may be less important than the others."

Labeling

Move: "Why must you be so stubborn?"

Countermove: "I don't think that calling each other names furthers our discussions. Perhaps we could stay with the issues."

Issue Expansion

Move: "Now that you brought that up, I would also like to mention . . . "

Countermove: "Let's finish the concern that I brought up first, then we can address some of yours."

Tackling

Move: "If you weren't so negligent, you would have seen another way."

Countermove: "Assigning blame is not the issue here. It does not matter who is at fault, but rather what we can do to rectify the mistake."

Reneging

Move: "I never said that. You must have misunderstood me."

Countermove: "Perhaps there was a miscommunication on both our parts. We need to be very clear, then, about what we are agreeing to do."

Backstabbing

Move: "You are going to take what *he* said seriously?"

Countermove: "I am just bringing to your attention what I have heard. To do otherwise would be dishonest of me."

Undermining

Move: "Sorry. I didn't mean to be late. It's just that something *important* came up."

Countermove: "You seem to be implying that what we are doing is not important. I would appreciate it if you could make an effort to be on time in the future."

Coalition Formation

Move: "There are many others who agree with me on this."

Countermove: "It would be better if you spoke only for yourself and let others speak for themselves as well."

Threats

Move: "If you don't let this go, I will be forced to do something neither of us will like."

Countermove: "It would indeed be unfortunate if things got out of control. I do not intend, however, to be guided by threats. It might be a lot more constructive if we could resolve this between us."

Each of these power tactics is used by people to control your behavior. You may have noticed some consistency in the ways that each manipulative ploy was countered by a more direct response, one that:

1. Labeled what was taking place
2. Let the other person know that you understood what was going on
3. Indicated your refusal to be baited on a personal level
4. Expressed your strong preference to move beyond blame
5. Communicated your preference to deal with issues
6. Acknowledged that each of you had the power to make things work or not
7. Clearly articulated your resolve not to back down
8. Stated your intent to address any future forms of manipulation with similar countermoves

People at work who are giving you trouble do not go away just because you ignore them. On the contrary, they may interpret your lack of response as acquiescence or surrender. Until you deal with them in a decisive way, they will continue to do whatever they are permitted to get away with.

The Need for Control

Manipulation is really just a means by which to maintain control. Whether through coercion or threat ("That's fine if you don't want to participate—I'll make sure the others know about your feelings.") or through guile, deception, charm, or guilt ("No, I don't mind if you don't come. I'll just go alone."), manipulation is used to get you to do things that you ordinarily would not do.

198

Not only does manipulation help unscrupulous individuals reach their goals, but it can help them control others. They feel powerful when they can restrict you from getting what you want or what you deserve. They love to blame you for standing in their way.

Bill has been established in his job for decades. He gets by on longevity rather than on competence. He perceives people all around him, most of whom are younger and ambitious, as nipping at his heels. He is not far wrong.

Bill uses all the guile and manipulative ploys at his disposal (and his resources in this area are formidable) to undermine or sabotage colleagues whom he perceives might be threats. Since from his perspective everyone is a potential competitor for power, Bill views life as an endless series of battles for control.

For example, Bill "befriended" one unsuspecting new employee with the intention of making certain this new threat was irreparably damaged. When his probationary contract was not extended, the young man had no idea that he had been blindsided by Bill. Another colleague, who was recently promoted, is undermined constantly by Bill, who spreads rumors and sets traps—and makes sure none of them can be traced back to him.

This is not organizational politics as usual: these are the actions of a threatened human being who thrives on power, whose principal motive in life is to control others and thereby give himself an illusion of internal control. He must be potent, after all. Look how he is feared, respected, and given a wide berth by others who are too gutless to take him on.

Even in a book such as this that emphasizes internal control and personal responsibility, it is important to recognize that there are limits to what is within your power to change. If you have a choice, Bill and others like him are not the kind of people you want to spend much time around. The problem is that sometimes you do not realize what you have gotten into until it is too late. You realize that the person you married, who lives in your home, who is in your family, who is your boss or partner or friend, is a person without a conscience, or is so desperate that he or she will do anything to get his or her way.

While these manipulative people may seem like agents of the devil sent to wreak havoc in your life, they are only trying to deal with their own pain. They are so afraid of intimacy, so mistrustful of others' intentions, perhaps so damaged inside that they seek to make others' lives as miserable as their own.

Keeping Your Goals in Mind

When you find yourself locked into a futile struggle in which your goals—and those of your adversary—are blocked, one of the options available to you is to redefine what it is that you want. Sometimes your original intentions become lost in the irrational desire to win an argument. You become so invested in the struggle that you are unable to back off enough to realize that the fight has become more important than the result.

In dissolving their business partnership, Dinah and Suzanne behaved like two people in the midst of an ugly divorce: they were interested not only in dividing up community property but also in inflicting some damage on one another. Each felt angry that the other one had not acted in their mutual interest. The two partners felt that perceived injustices must be righted before they could go their separate ways.

Dinah and Suzanne argued for days about who would keep

the stationery, then for weeks about who would retain what furniture. Outside observers, such as their spouses and secretary, looked on with horrified bemusement. They had been such good friends, and now they were fighting over trivial matters as if their lives were at stake. It was beause they had been dear, trusting friends as well as partners that they were having so much trouble letting go. At the same time they were disassembling their business, a not insurmountable challenge, they were also trying to work through their ambivalent feelings, a process that would take years to complete.

When children separate from their parents, when spouses divorce, when friends or partners go their separate ways, it is useful to feel a certain amount of animosity—it helps us deal with the sense of loss we experience. In the case of Dinah and Suzanne, they were attempting to deal with practical concerns at the same time they were trying to work through their unresolved feelings of sadness, hurt, anger, and resentment. They lost sight of what they were negotiating for in the first place, so embroiled were they in their heated arguments.

Since it was not reasonable to expect that they could deal with their unfinished emotional business at the same time they were dissolving their business arrangement, they made a pact (at the urging of their secretary) to complete the latter before they got into the former.

Express Feeling and Content

Most internal reactions are composed of two parts, each of which demands equal attention. The *content* of communication refers to the actual issues you are talking about—who will do what, what the problem is, what it is that you want that you are not

201

getting. Without addressing underlying feelings, however, communication is likely to end with unfinished business that will permeate the next exchange.

This was exactly the state of affairs between Heidi and Samantha, two associates who work together in the same office. For months, Heidi had been simmering on low boil, her feelings about the way she had been treated by Samantha affecting not only her concentration at work but also her sleep. "It isn't really such a big deal," Heidi told herself. "I am a professional. I don't let this stuff bother me."

Spouting the credo of a man's world, in which feelings are presumed to be irrelevant to conducting the business at hand, Heidi tried very hard to be the consummate professional, dealing with the content of issues while stuffing the accompanying feelings.

Although I had the opportunity to speak only with Heidi about this situation, I am fairly certain that Samantha must have felt much the same way—locked into conflict with a perceived adversary in which both parties refused to give themselves, or each other, permission to express their feelings of hurt and resentment along with a discussion of the content.

It is ironic that even as adults we often have to go to other people, sometimes therapists, in order to get permission to do things we want to do, things we know we must do. In Heidi's case, my role was easy.

"Just because the atmosphere in your office is dominated by traditional unhealthy norms of pretending you are a cold-blooded reptile without emotion does not mean you will lose all credibility and respect if you acknowledge that you do have feelings. And if that were the case, would you want to stay in a place where you cannot be yourself, where you must disown the most important parts of who you are?

"What is particularly interesting about your ongoing dispute with Samantha is that you sense she is feeling the same pressure you are—to excel in a man's world by imitating men. If you are asking me to give you permission to be more like the way you are outside the office—that is, with the full range of your expressiveness as a thinking and feeling person—I cannot do that. But you can."

Ultimately, Heidi did find a place for herself that allowed her to be more genuinely expressive. Unfortunately, when she finally began telling Samantha how she felt as well as what she thought, the feelings she had been holding inside for so long tumbled out in a seemingly endless stream. She expressed not only her hurt and pain but also the realization that she felt stifled—the job was killing her. Samantha felt so threatened by this honest disclosure that she retreated even further into her professional shell. When we processed the encounter afterwards, Heidi readily confessed that the reason she had been so reluctant to get into her feelings was that she knew they would lead to action she was not yet ready to initiate—seeking employment elsewhere.

Heidi's dilemma illustrates the importance of defining just how motivated you are to follow your heart as well as your head when you do confront obstacles that are blocking what you want. Expressing yourself fully does not come without certain risks. This task is also not one that you were born knowing how to do. Expressing yourself clearly, fully, and powerfully depends on developing some very specific skills. As we will discuss in Chapter Ten, even under those conditions, there are still a number of conflicts you will be able to do little about.

When Conflicts Can't Be Resolved

EVEN THE MOST ELABORATE and well-thought-out plans do not always work. The process presented in this book for working through conflict by counteracting tendencies toward blame is quite effective for many—but not all—circumstances and situations. Despite your best intentions and most dedicated efforts, not all conflicts can be worked through.

Some Differences Are Irreconcilable

Some long-term internal patterns are irreversible, based on unresolved issues from the past that can never really be laid to rest completely. Even in the present, when two people feel strongly enough about something, when their whole belief systems are predicated on one particular opinion or action, even small changes are unlikely. A staunch Republican and Democrat are unlikely to agree on affirmative action policies or right-to-life issues. Two individuals whose most basic principles lead them in opposite directions are unlikely to find common ground in which to negotiate a truce.

Ned believes that human beings are basically evil and untrustworthy, that people have to be monitored closely or they will easily be led astray. Furthermore, people will lie every chance they get and are only out for their own interests. By contrast, Sidney believes in the basic goodness of humankind. He feels that, given sufficient support and encouragement, people will do what is right. Most people can be trusted; the ones who do evil things are the exception rather than the rule.

Now imagine that Ned and Sidney are in roughly equal positions of power—as friends, partners, co-workers, siblings, or committee members. Suppose an issue comes up related to what to do about a third person, whose actions will affect them both. Conflict between Ned and Sidney inevitably will arise, just as it does every time they discuss anything important, because their basic belief systems are polar opposites.

NED: We've got to do something about this situation, protect ourselves as much as possible.

SIDNEY: Let's just see what happens. It will all work out for the best.

NED: You can be so naive. Unless we assume the worst, and act accordingly, we are going to be short-changed and vulnerable.

SIDNEY: If you continue to believe that, it will be so. I would rather give him the benefit of the doubt, just as I would like him to treat me.

NED: I just can't go along with that. I *won't* do it. You can do whatever you want but I'm going to take some protective steps.

SIDNEY: Do whatever you need to do. I can understand that.

NED: Damn, I hate it when you talk like that.

SIDNEY: I feel the same way about you.

This is a conversation that these two antagonists have played out a hundred different times in a hundred different ways. If anything, over time each has become even more firmly entrenched in his position, more thoroughly convinced that he is right and the other is wrong. When Sidney tries to uncover the underlying reasons for their conflicts, the sources of their antagonism, the roots of his own determination to take the positions he does, he concludes that he and Ned are so fundamentally different in their basic beliefs and values and in the ways they perceive the world that conflict between them is unavoidable no matter what they do. Sidney no longer blames Ned for the way he is, nor does he blame himself for the problems; he realizes, instead, that when two people feel as differently about things as they do, conflict is the logical result. In order to resolve their difficulties, one of them would have to abandon a position that is a fundamental part of his very being.

Every time Sidney commits himself to act differently, he comes up against the same wall, the familiar realization that their differences are irreconcilable. Each time he tries out different strategies for dealing with Ned, he discovers all over again that they rarely agree on what courses of action to take. That is not to say, of course, that Sidney and Ned cannot negotiate a truce based on the awareness of their basic conflict. Given their differences in orientation, however, the best they can strive for is to reduce the intensity of their struggles so that they both stop allowing themselves to feel so wounded every time they deal with one another.

Applying the methods described in the book, Sidney accepts the fact that he cannot resolve his conflicts with Ned. Furthermore, he realizes that he does not even *want* to. As you will recall from the discussion in Chapter Seven on the positive functions of conflict, it is the act of struggling that helps you clarify your most cherished beliefs. Every time Sidney goes up against Ned in an argument, he may leave the exchange feeling frustrated and misunderstood, but he also likes the feeling that he now has a firmer grasp of what issues he feels most strongly about. Ned may be his greatest nemesis, but he is also one of his best teachers in the sense that he is provoked into achieving deeper levels of understanding about himself, about others, and about the world.

Even when conflicts cannot be resolved, when the disagreements between you and someone else are based on fundamental, core differences in your basic beliefs and styles, there still is much you can do to live with these experiences in such a way that they become instructive rather than destructive. The ability to do this is based on the particular meaning you decide to assign to the exchange. Note, for example, two different ways in which Sidney can decide to think about his interactions with Ned:

"What a pain that I have to deal with him! *[Exaggerating the degree of annoyance only makes things worse.]* Why can't he be more reasonable *[more like me]*? I have never known anyone who is so rigid, so unyielding in the positions that he takes. *[Blame. Judging others by your own standards.]* I dread the time we have to spend together. *[Expectations will dictate the results.]* I just know he is going to try to get me again. *[He is just defending his own beliefs in the same way that you are.]* These fights serve no useful purpose. They are a complete waste of time *[From this perspective, that is assuredly true.]*"

Contrast the previous inner dialogue with one in which Sidney attempts to accept the inevitability of a certain amount of conflict with Ned but prefers to think differently about the meaning of these encounters.

"These interactions I have with Ned sure are interesting! [*Use of neutral word* interesting *to describe the experience.*] This is certainly an unusual experience for me to become so passionately committed during an exchange. [*Valuing the uniqueness.*] In a sense, we bring out the worst in one another, but also the best. [*A balanced perspective recognizing how conflict is instructive.*] I wonder what it is about our respective styles that seems to ignite such heated exchanges? [*Thoughtful reflection on the meaning of the behavior.*] I suspect there are some things I might do a bit differently so that I don't aggravate matters but still maintain the purity of my positions. [*A problem-solving mode with realistic goals.*] I certainly don't look forward to these arguments, but I recognize that after each one is over, I have learned something about myself and others that I could not have learned any other way. [*Conceptualizing the experience as constructive rather than destructive.*]"

Even when you face individuals with whom it is clear that resolving basic conflicts is out of the question, you still can apply the methods previously described to reduce the suffering you experience and to make the best of the situation.

Agreement Is Sometimes Not Worth the Effort

Some conflicts are so complex, so enduring, or so ambiguous, that it is impossible to sort out all the variables involved, much less put together a plan for reaching consensus. When the cost of getting along in terms of investment of time and energy is greater than the perceived gains, it is sometimes better to accept a low-grade, chronic dispute as within acceptable limits of tolerance.

Madeline and Ernestine, although they feel a certain grudging affection for one another, have been bickering as long as they have been neighbors. Neither of them has experienced this kind of relationship before, since they both enjoy a wide network of friends with whom they get along fine.

Over the years they have tried to smooth out their differences. Mutual friends have attempted to act as intermediaries. At least once a month they meet for coffee or lunch; more often they speak over the fence. But each knows all too well that underneath the cordial pleasantness there is a major fight waiting to break out. Each time they have tried to figure out why they get on each other's nerves, they have only made things worse. Without explicitly saying so, they have agreed that it is no longer worth the effort to resolve their differences or to find out what is at their source. Instead, they tread lightly around each other, stay away from controversial subjects, and maintain an uneasy distance.

This attitude of "it's not worth it" also can be used as an excuse for avoiding the effort that is involved in making a relationship work. Still, it is up to you to decide with whom you are willing to tolerate a degree of conflict. It is one thing to avoid working through a minor dispute with a neighbor you do not have to see if you so choose; it is quite another to try to do so with someone with whom you live or work or to whom you feel close.

Madeline has decided that it is not worth her time and energy to pursue an intimate friendship with Ernestine, who is not a significant person in her life. She applies the method previously described in such a way as to keep this relationship in perspective: "Even when we are fighting about one thing or another, I try never to forget that our arguments are really not that important. It really isn't worth it for me to get all upset or lose sleep over this stuff. This really helps me shrug things off pretty quickly so that I don't hold a grudge the next time we run into one another."

On the other hand, Madeline is also in constant conflict with her husband of twenty-six years. They fight over who is lazier, who gets to hold the remote control, and—the most vicious of all their battles—who has betrayed the other most severely. Madeline has told herself in this case also that it is not worth the struggle to try and work on a more loving, cooperative relationship. But this time she uses this explanation as an excuse for avoiding the risks that would be involved in confronting her fears of intimacy. She finds it much easier to blame her husband as a "stubborn old coot," throw up her hands in exasperation, and tell anyone who will listen that nothing will ever change. And, of course, nothing *will* change if that is what she believes.

Madeline may be correct in her assumption that after twenty-six years together perhaps she and her husband will never get along like they did as newlyweds. She also may be correct in her assessment that continual conflict is a part of the way they relate to one another. Given that they have tried marriage counseling a few times, and that their children have tried without success to act as mediators, maybe arguing is simply one way that they express affection to one another. Many individuals who are afraid of the vulnerability associated with allowing themselves to become close to people argue as a way to keep others at a safe distance (remember the positive function of conflict as a regulator of distance?).

Madeline and her husband really do care for each other very much (I have it on good authority since, as one of their marriage counselors, I spent considerable time in their company). Fighting, bickering, and arguing have become ways for them to relate to one another in an intimate way (conflicts *are* intimate, after all) without having to risk getting hurt too badly. They learned long ago how to protect themselves during conflicts so that neither sustained any real damage. In fact, their fights are a lot more disturbing to others around them than they are upsetting to them. Madeline and her husband have learned to accommodate themselves to a level of battle, not unlike citizens who lived in France during the Hundred Years War or in Vietnam in the twentieth century.

When Madeline used the excuse, "It's not worth the effort," what she really meant to express was, "I am afraid of doing anything different." You must make a similar distinction in those situations in which it *appears* as if a conflict is not worth the trouble of addressing it. Are you telling yourself this in order to save yourself further aggravation, or rather to avoid the hard work and risks associated with confronting your fears? Only you can answer this question, but before you decide it may help you to get some input from others who know both you and the situation well.

Some Choices Are Mutually Exclusive

You will not be able to settle a dispute, at least immediately, with someone who is a competitor for the same prize. When two people are vying for the same goal—a promotion, a lover, an award, limited money or resources—and no compromise is possible, there is going to be one winner and one loser. This situation is quite conducive to conflict; in fact, competition is designed to maximize the struggle—spectators consider it entertaining.

212

In a situation where one person gets what she wants and the other person does not, conflict and resentment are part of the consequences, at least for a while. Christy and Marcel have been settled in their careers ever since they were married. Christy has been offered a major promotion in another city, which she has decided she cannot pass up. Marcel must choose between joining her in the move, thereby setting his own career back many years, or staying where he is, thereby ending their relationship. For simplicity's sake, assume that they are not looking for a reason to split apart and that compromise is not possible.

No matter what the outcome of their decision, whether Christy takes the job or not, whether Marcel joins her or stays behind, conflict is likely to persist for some time. At least during an interim stage, they both will need to accommodate to a degree of tension and disagreement until they can resolve their differences.

The problem in these situations is often not that you did not get what you wanted but that the way you react *afterward* is conducive to continued suffering. So what if this time you were not able to get your way? Yes, I know, this time it was *really* important. You have *never* wanted anything so badly. The point is: what are you going to do about it now? You can't change what has already happened. You can't (I assume) redefine the win-lose situation to one in which both of you can get what you want. The bottom line is that you can't have what you want this time. Now you must decide how long you want to feel sorry for yourself and how much you want to castigate yourself or blame the other person for acting unfairly.

Even during conflicts in which the choices are mutually exclusive and you end up on the short end of the exchange, you still have tremendous latitude in how deeply you decide (and it *is* a decision) to feel wounded by the experience. In the example presented earlier, Marcel did pout for a while, hoping that Christy might feel sorry for him and call off her plans. Once he realized that there was little he could do to change her mind and even less he could do to alter what had transpired previously, Marcel decided that he would make the best of the situation. After he was able to let go of his resentment, stop feeling like a helpless victim, and get on with the options that were available to him, Marcel was able to negotiate with Christy some concessions that would make his transition easier. Just as important, he was able to negotiate with himself in such a way that he no longer felt like an embittered loser in their relationship.

There Is No Solution

When I am working with clients, I never ask, "What is your problem?" Instead I prefer the alternative term *concern* or *issue*. Using the term *problem* implies that there is a solution, usually a best one, just like we learned in math class. In the realm of human struggles, however, there is no guarantee that any particular difficulty has a solution, and especially not a "best" one that can be determined easily. Life is a puzzle, and sometimes pieces are missing, or the pieces we are given do not fit together properly. Even after we work so hard to fashion together a finished puzzle, it may not remotely resemble what we thought it would look like.

There is stress associated with Jose's mother moving into the home he shares with his wife, Lopita. The mother has a progressive, degenerative nervous disorder that predisposes her to be even more demanding and irrational than is her usual formidable manner. The couple's otherwise serene life-style is disrupted in a significant way by the presence of the sick mother, who continuously lashes out at Lopita, demanding attention and criticizing her every chance she gets. Any attempt by Lopita and Jose to calm down the elderly lady, to respond to her inappropriate outbursts, is like trying to stop a hurricane—even if she wanted to alter her behavior, she would be unable to do so because of the degree of perceptual and cognitive distortion brought on by her disease.

Neither Jose nor Lopita has other family members who could help share the burden. Cultural values related to taking care of aging parents, in tandem with a tight financial situation, make it impossible to send the mother elsewhere; they have no choice but to live together. Harmony among them is out of the question.

They can partition off the house as much as possible. Jose and Lopita can also support one another as they try to enforce some limits. In spite of their best efforts, however, they must live with a certain degree of conflict in their home. There is no solution to their problem other than to learn to endure the discomfort in such a way that they minimize its effects on their relationship.

Living with Futility

It is fruitless to assume that every interpersonal conflict can be worked through—that if only you were better prepared, if you knew more or were more highly skilled, then you could make things better.

I feel much this same way as I approach any new challenging therapy case. I assume that, given enough time and patience, anyone can be helped—if not by me, then certainly by someone else. It is a rude awakening for me every time I face an individual who does not improve no matter how hard I try to be helpful or what I do to try to make a difference. At first, I assume it is some inadequacy in me—if only I were smarter, better trained, more sensitive and perceptive; if I had attended more workshops, were surrounded by brighter colleagues; if only I were more skilled at what I do, then surely I could figure out what is going wrong and rectify it.

This misguided belief neglects to include the reality that: (1) No matter how talented and well prepared I might be, there is no way I can reach everyone all of the time. (2) Not everyone really wants to change, no matter what they might say. Sometimes the payoffs of their dysfunction and behavior are too attractive or they just don't want to do the hard work that is involved. (3) Some people are not good candidates for therapy. They lack insight or motivation or sufficient patience to proceed through the process.

I have been told by supervisors and colleagues (even professional reviewers who edit my books) that I tend to inflate my own role in the process of helping someone else change—I don't have as much power and influence as I think I do.

There comes a time when we all have to come to terms with what is in our domain that we are in a position to do something about and what is out of our control. With respect to the former, there are quite a number of actions we can take, and internal guidance we can offer ourselves, that will reduce if not eliminate any conflict. As to the latter predicament of feeling futility and helplessness, there are things we can do to learn to live with that as well.

Part of learning to think more constructively about conflicts in your life is to recognize realistically what is within your power to change and what is not. As you have heard throughout the process described in this book, rather than blaming others for not cooperating with your preferences, it is far more useful to take inventory of all the things that you have tried that do not work and, rather than repeating them, try something else.

Flexibility Is the Key

The key to planning strategy in any human struggle, whether on the battlefield or the football field, whether it involves a political election, a debate, or an interpersonal dispute, is to plan an overall set of tactics for the engagement and then be prepared to improvise as the situation changes. Whereas previously we have concentrated mostly on what you can do inside your own head to conceptualize conflicts differently, or to understand the motives that drive your self-defeating actions, I would like to summarize some principles to keep in mind before you decide that a conflict cannot be resolved. This problem-solving strategy is based on several assumptions that are compatible with the method introduced to you in this book.

1. *A solution is possible that will be satisfactory to both parties.* As you have seen, this may not always be the case.
2. *This resolution can be negotiated within reasonable time parameters.* Pragmatic concerns do dictate what can be done.
3. *Both participants will have to give up something in order to*

achieve their mutual goals. This implies that both participants are interested in compromise.

4. *Collaboration and cooperation are preferred over fighting for
   competing interests.* This assumption holds true only
   when both participants have accepted that they will not
   get all of what they want.

5. *The focus should remain on the problem at hand rather than
   on assigning blame as to who is at fault.* Staying with the
   agenda is crucial to avoid lapsing into name-calling.

6. *The greater the flexibility in both participants, the more likely
   it is that a mutually satisfying resolution of the conflict will
   take place.* Flexibility must be evenly balanced in order
   for both people to end up feeling satisfied.

7. *An attitude of objectivity and systematic inquiry is more
   effective than personalizing the issues.* Stay calm rather
   than losing control.

8. *Participants operate as partners who are equally vested in
   making sure that both are pleased with the compromise that
   is worked out.* This may very well be the most difficult
   task of all between two people who are actively involved in conflict.

9. *Make sure that you deal with not only the present struggle
   but also the underlying issues from the past that are sparking
   such intense emotional responses.* If you have progressed
   through the internal process described earlier in this
   book, this task will make it much easier for you to address
   the whole conflict instead of just a few of its parts.

When a conflict cannot be resolved, it is most likely because the assumptions just described are absent. Therefore, if

your intent is to try and work things out with someone, you will wish to review the rules under which you are operating. Before you attempt any active intervention, or decide whether to give up, it will be helpful for you to include in the last stage (described in Chapter Six on experimenting with alternative strategies) as many of these assumptions as possible. In any negotiation participants must agree on the ground rules before they ever approach the problems at hand.

Although a problem-solving mode is preferred as a first choice, it is by no means the optimal style of conflict resolution in all situations. Andrew, for example, has tried repeatedly to negotiate in this style with his ex-wife, Marna, over visitation rights related to their children. During those times when he has demonstrated maximum flexibility, fairness, and cooperation, Andrew has consistently ended up on the losing side of the transaction. As long as they are unable to agree on the rules of their negotiations, which involve inflicting hurt on one another as much as any attempt to find a solution to their lingering problems, a cooperative strategy does not work very well.

In fact, no set of tactics seems to work well more than once. Each time they face one another at the bargaining table over who gets the kids for the holidays, protracted arguments left over from their conflicted marriage continue to dominate. In this situation, the best strategy is one in which the participants protect themselves as best they can. They will both try anything and everything to get the upper hand—threats, avoidance, manipulation, guilt, emotional blackmail—whatever works. The problem is that everyone loses: Andrew, Marna, and, most of all, their children, who are caught in the middle.

An outside mediator eventually helped them demonstrate more concern for the present problem—parental sharing of visitation rights—than for acting out their resentments. There will be times when you, too, may wish to bring in a neutral third party to help you negotiate a resolution of a conflict. The strategies employed in mediation are based on principles that you may wish to adopt as your own operating guides. The following suggestions also may be incorporated into the way you think about approaching conflict situations.

1. *Work within an atmosphere of cooperation. If such a climate does not exist, do what it takes to create it.* In order to accomplish this, you will need to apply what you learned in the first few stages of the conflict resolution process—what undermines your trust, what buttons of yours are being pushed, and what are the origins (both in your past and in the history of your relationship with the other person) of these difficulties.

2. *Remain as flexible as possible in your approach, altering your style according to the changing circumstances.* Flexibility is possible only if you have fully worked through the resentments that have been getting in your way. When you have taken responsibility for your own role in the problem without blaming yourself or others (Chapter Four), you are much better positioned to address grievances in a flexible way.

3. *Make sure that strong emotions are dealt with before attempts are made to deal with the issues.* Your feelings must be processed internally before you attempt to express them externally. Only after you have sorted out what part of your reaction is the result of your own unre-

solved issues can you begin to figure out the emotional issues embedded in the present struggle. Always look inward first, then look outside yourself for clues.

4. *Negotiate from a position of strength and trust. Only after the second betrayal should you resort to self-interest strategies.* Part of experimenting with alternative strategies (Chapter Six) involves starting out from one angle and then abandoning it only after you are sure it does not work. Starting from a position of trust rather than suspicion does not place you in as vulnerable a situation as you might think—unless you fail to make adjustments in light of evidence that your adversary is not trustworthy.

5. *Communicate clearly during the negotiations. Make sure that you are understood and that you understand what the other person wants.* In order to be understood, you will first need to understand what it is that you want. As you have already learned, that takes a considerable amount of self-reflection. It is equally important to get outside of yourself enough to be sensitive to the other person's preferences so that you may address them effectively.

6. *Block repetitive negative interaction patterns by changing the structure* (place, time, methods, control, climate, and so on) *of the negotiations.* This is part of any action strategy. Pay close attention to what you are doing, what effect it is having. Note what the other person does and what impact this behavior is having on you. Study the patterns of circular causality (mentioned in Chapter Two) so that you can identify what is maintaining the dysfunctional interaction. Then change what you do in some way!

7. *Encourage a positive frame of mind in which you convey the*

commitment to work things out. When you communicate your interest in resolving a dispute, especially in clear, explicit ways, you invite the other person to join you as a partner. Committing yourself to act differently (Chapter Five) involves conveying to the other person your determination to work things out. If he or she is not interested in cooperating with your efforts, so be it. But you have indicated your resolve that, one way or the other, you are going to leave the exchange satisfied with your own role in the process.

8. *Make it safe to disagree without jeopardizing the relationship or the outcome.* When you have successfully moved through the various stages, you will no longer feel personally threatened by the interaction. You have, after all, neutralized the noxious effects of the past. Resolving differences frequently involves taking risks (Chapter Five). That means disagreeing with one another, debating constructively, ironing out differences through honest dialogue. This can take place only when you can express yourself without undue fear of being offended or offensive.

9. *Stick with the agreed-upon agenda rather than letting yourselves become distracted by insignificant issues.* Whether dealing with conflicts in love, at work, or anywhere else, it is crucial that things not be allowed to deteriorate to the point where irrelevant, distracting issues are brought into the discussion. During productive conflict resolution, one or both of you will sometimes be required to ask the questions: Are we on task? Is what we are doing right now helping us get to where we would like to be?

10. *Avoid even the appearance of blame.* No surprise here. This *is*, after all, the main theme of this book. Interwoven throughout every stage in the book's process have been reminders as to how important it is that you move beyond blame if you are ever to resolve interpersonal disputes.

There is nothing that will sabotage any strategy you employ more quickly than the mere suggestion that you are blaming the other person for the troubles. Equally detrimental is for you to accept blame that is directed toward you. This compliance tactic (perhaps even driven by the misguided belief that one person can be at fault in a conflict) will only encourage further fault-finding in the future. When either party in a dispute is feeling defensive, the inevitable consequence of blame, any strategy that is selected by a mediator or by yourself is doomed to fail.

Getting Help from a Professional

There comes a time when people may reach an impasse they cannot break through without outside assistance. It is not so much that professional help, in the form of a consultant, mediator, or therapist, is necessary in order to resolve difficult disputes, but it can make things progress much more quickly.

The same thing holds true with hiring any expert. Given enough time, study, and motivation, you could certainly fill out your own tax returns, handle your own legal affairs, or hook up your own water heater, but often it is much more efficient to hire someone to provide assistance.

In the field of conflict resolution, getting help from a professional can accomplish several things you would find it difficult to do yourself. It can:

1. Bring an objective, neutral, unbiased perspective to the negotiations, the perspective of someone without a vested interest in the outcome. Theoretically, such a professional does not care how the dispute is settled as long as both parties are satisfied.
2. Introduce fresh ways of looking at your problems, sometimes even redefining them in ways that make them easier to solve.
3. Facilitate a more orderly, rational, purposeful approach to settling the dispute.
4. Help participants hear one another, understand each other's points of view, and respond to what each person has said.
5. Clarify underlying issues that are getting in the way of understanding or action.
6. Initiate more of a commitment to change on the part of all those concerned.
7. Present methods and strategies designed to disrupt usual dysfunctional patterns and force participants to discover healthier ways of interacting.
8. Initiate adjustments in the "system" that control the ways that participants relate to one another. This includes realigning the distribution of power, the coalitions that have formed, the rigid boundaries that interfere with effective communication.
9. Suggest resources that might prove helpful to participants in their search for common ground. This could

include readings, homework assignments, or prescribed tasks designed to facilitate better communication.

Ordinarily, we think of services such as those just described as being most appropriate for marital conflicts, divorce mediation, or child custody disputes. There is no reason, however, why a supervisor and subordinate, two friends, two partners, a parent and a child, might not also consult a professional to get some help.

"What I liked best about seeing a counselor to help us work out a new arrangement in our partnership is that it was safe for us to talk about things that really bothered us. If we tried to negotiate in the office, even with a third party present, one or the other of us would lose control and start screaming. If the counselor did nothing else, he was an impartial witness. Besides, his office had thin walls so he wouldn't let us raise our voices during discussions. I think that helped most of all."

Even an Amateur Can Help

Although professional assistance has the advantage of providing a truly impartial, neutral mediator, sometimes it is not feasible to have an outsider involved. Perhaps both parties are not amenable to seeing a counselor or consultant—it may be too expensive, or perhaps one person feels it is a sign of weakness to ask for help. It also can be difficult finding a person whom both people feel is qualified, competent, and trustworthy. In some situations, it is impractical to take the argument out of its natural setting and relocate it to a professional office.

For whatever the reason that professional help will not work, friends or associates often can provide support. Even if they cannot mediate the dispute itself, they can help in other ways. During times when you feel discouraged they can suggest alternative courses of action. They can offer valuable feedback on the situation or on your interpersonal style. Most of all, they can help prop up your confidence. No matter what the outcome of the conflict, it feels good to know that your most trusted allies will still be there for you.

This informal "amateur" help crops up in every organization and setting—in teachers' lounges, employee cafeterias, kitchens, and phone calls with friends. The key point is that when you are in conflict with someone, it is even more important than usual for you to be able to talk about what you find upsetting and to process it. If you don't have a safe place to nurse your wounds and build up your strength and resolve, you need to recruit more supportive individuals in your life. You cannot fight alone and expect to keep up your morale.

Applying the Book's Methods in the Most Difficult of Situations

A woman calls me for a first appointment. Before I meet with her, could I please contact the referring therapist, who has a lot of family background that I might find useful? I tell her that I would prefer to meet her first to form my own first impression, but she makes her request a nonnegotiable condition.

She begins our first session with the question: "So what did the therapist say about me?"

"Nothing much. She doesn't really know you except through your children. She did mention that you may meddle a bit too much in their lives."

Before I know what has hit me, the woman is standing and

screaming at me: "You call yourself a therapist? How can you take someone else's opinion . . . "

"Wait a minute," I try to interject. "I didn't say I took what she said at face value. She said she didn't know you."

"That's what you say, but you never should have contacted her in the first place."

"But you asked me to talk to her before I saw you."

"Hey, hotshot, you're the expert. *You* should know better. You should have told me."

Blame. Blame. Blame. I can hear it ringing in my ears. She will not look at how she has manipulated this situation so she can be a victim. She is trying to . . . Oops. Now I am trying to do it, too—trying to blame her for getting under my skin. I even try a little underhanded manipulation myself, giving her my best omnipotent "shrink look" and saying in buttery tones: "You seem to want to blame me for putting you in a defensive position regarding meddling in your children's lives. It seems to me that that comment would not bother you so much if it had not hit the mark."

I feel smug. Put her in her place, I did. But not for long. In another moment we are arguing again about something else. It is clear to me that this relationship will not work, although I feel muddled as to why. Sometimes you just can't sort out why and how you keep ending up in conflict with someone; the dynamics are too complex to understand fully. It is enough to realize that you must protect yourself since you are unlikely to be successful in getting the other person to change her behavior.

In twenty years of practice, this was the first client I ever "fired." I told her that I would not work with her. Even that led to an argument: the more I insisted that our relationship was too conflicted to be therapeutic, the more she became determined that I was the best professional for her. She accused me of secretly admiring her manipulative abilities to protect herself, because she was far better at the game than I was: "What's the matter, Doc? Can't you take the heat? Just because I argue with you and don't accept everything you say, does that mean you can't work with me? Am I too threatening to your ego?"

She was not far wrong. I *did* admire her skill as a manipulator, all the while I was aghast at her impact on me. I might not have been able to do much to resolve the conflicts between us, but I surely could do a few things to limit the negative effects, not the least of which was to deny her access to me in the future. I also had considerable work to do in order to put this experience in perspective so that I could learn from what happened, as well as limit the lingering feelings that were most disturbing.

Yes, you know what comes next. I asked myself what it was about her, and the ways that she treated me, that got under my skin so easily. It did not take very deep excavations to figure out that she threatened my need for control (that is, after all, why I became a therapist in the first place). I also realized that because I could not immediately make sense of what she was trying to do, I became impatient, pushing her in ways for which she was not yet ready.

Armed with this awareness of both my personal and interpersonal issues that were being triggered, I could more easily take some responsibility for what had happened. Perhaps this woman was indeed a very difficult person for most anyone to deal with, but I was fairly difficult myself—a fact I did not like to admit even to myself. This discomfort worked to my advantage in motivating me to do a few things differently. In this case, it was a moot point as to what I did with this particular woman (who, I gleefully reminded myself, I would never see again); what was most important to me was discovering the other conflicts in my life that had followed (and will follow) a similar pattern.

A few weeks later a colleague and I got into a dispute over some issue that seemed important at the time. Although he did not resemble the woman I just described in any obvious way, my feelings during the interaction felt very familiar. Indeed (surprise!), the same issues of control reared their ugly heads once again. This time, however, I was prepared. I even knew what I was looking for.

The solution in this particular situation involved more than a reminder to myself about what was taking place. I took the risk of bringing the matter out into the open by confronting the person about how resentful I felt at his efforts to control me. He, of course, had his own perspective on the situation, which was different from mine. Since we both were quite interested in resolving this dispute, we followed many of the assumptions described earlier in this chapter. Most helpful of all was the mutual belief that we could work things out, that we were not going to stop the discussions until both of us felt all right.

It was interesting for me to realize that it was the so-called difficult client I described earlier who was actually responsible for helping me discover some painful aspects of my interpersonal functioning. During this time we have spent together, you will have noticed my strong preference to try and find some value, some constructive purpose, in even the most noxious of experiences. Because I tend to look for things that I can use to help both myself and my clients, you would naturally expect that I find exactly what I am searching for.

I am utterly convinced, beyond a shadow of a doubt, that conflicted relationships are not the scourges of our lives but the price of admission we pay for living with other people. I do not deny that conflict is unpleasant, that it is uncomfortable, that it forces us to confront some very painful issues in our lives. But there is no better way for us to get closer to ourselves and become more intimate with others.

About the Author

JEFFREY A. KOTTLER is professor of counseling and educational psychology at the University of Nevada, Las Vegas. He has worked as a therapist in a variety of settings—including hospitals, mental health centers, schools, clinics, universities, corporations, and private practice. Jeffrey is an internationally recognized authority in the area of human relationships, having authored thirteen books on the subjects of teaching and therapy.

Recommended Reading

Ardrey, R. (1967). *The territorial imperative*. London: Collins.

Argyle, M., & Furnham, A. (1983). Sources of satisfaction and conflict in long-term relationships. *Journal of Marriage and the Family*, August, 481–493.

Axelrod, R. (1984). *The evolution of cooperation*. New York: Basic Books.

Blalock, H. M. (1989). *Power and conflict*. Newbury Park, CA: Sage.

Bulman, R., & Wortman, C. B. (1977). Attributions of blame and coping in the "real world": Severe accident victims react to their lot. *Journal of Personality and Social Psychology*, *35*, 351–363.

Crosby, J. F. (1980). Responsibility for feelings: A multilateral approach to causation. *Journal of Marital and Family Therapy*, October, 439–446.

Deutsch, M. (1973). *The resolution of conflict*. New Haven, CT: Yale University Press.

Dudgeon, C. (1992). Thwart office terrorists with these tactics. *Chicago Tribune*, November 8.

Duncan, B. L., & Rock, J. W. (1993). Saving relationships: The power of the unpredictable. *Psychology Today*, Jan./Feb.

Elias, M. (1981). Serum cortisol, testosterone, and testosterone-binding globulin responses to competitive fighting in human males. *Aggressive Behavior*, *7*, 215–224.

Evans, P. (1992). *The verbally abusive relationship*. Holbrook, MA: Bob Adams.

233

Folger, J. P., Poole, M. S., & Stutman, R. K. (1993). *Working through conflict.* New York: HarperCollins.

Goffman, E. (1957). *Presentation of self in everyday life.* New York: Doubleday.

Harris, M. (1977). *Cannibals and kings: The origins of cultures.* New York: Vintage Books.

Hart, B. H. L. (1967). *Strategy.* New York: New American Library.

Heitler, S. (1990). *From conflict to resolution.* New York: Norton.

Kottler, J. A. (1990). *Private moments, secret selves: Enriching your time alone.* New York: Ballantine.

Kottler, J. A. (1992). *Compassionate therapy: Working with difficult clients.* San Francisco: Jossey-Bass.

Kottler, J. A. (1993). *On being a therapist* (2nd ed.). San Francisco: Jossey-Bass.

Kottler, J. A., & Blau, D. S. (1989). *The imperfect therapist: Learning from failure in therapeutic practice.* San Francisco: Jossey-Bass.

LoPate, P. (1989). *Against joie de vivre.* New York: Simon & Schuster.

Lorenz, K. (1966). *On aggression.* New York: Bantam.

Maynard, D. W. (1985). On the function of social conflict among children. *American Sociological Review, 50,* 207–223.

Maynard-Smith, J. (1982). *Evolution and the theory of games.* Cambridge, MA: Cambridge University Press.

Mills, J., & Chusmir, L. H. (1988). Managerial and conflict resolution styles: Work and home differences. *Journal of Social Behavior and Personality, 3,* 303–316.

Moore, C. W. (1991). *The mediation process: Practical strategies for resolving conflicts.* San Francisco: Jossey-Bass.

Ogley, R. (1991). *Conflict under the microscope.* Aldershot, England: Avebury.

Patchen, M. (1988). *Resolving disputes between nations.* Durham, NC: Duke University Press.

Pruitt, D. G., & Rubin, J. Z. (1986). *Social conflict: Escalation, stalemate, and settlement.* New York: Random House.

Rapoport, A. (1960). *Fights, games, and debates.* Ann Arbor: University of Michigan Press.

Rice, P. L. (1992). *Stress and health.* Pacific Grove, CA: Brooks/Cole.

Robarchek, C. A. (1979). Conflict, emotion, and abreaction: Resolution of conflict among the Semai Senoi. *Ethos,* 104–123.

Rubin, J., & Rubin, C. (1989). *When families fight*. New York: William Morrow.

Scott, G. G. (1990). *Resolving conflict*. Oakland, CA: New Harbinger.

Shantz, C. (1987). Conflicts between children. *Child Development, 58*, 283–305.

Shaver, K. G. (1985). *The attribution of blame*. New York: Springer-Verlag.

Sillars, A., & Parry, D. (1982). Stress, cognition, and communication in interpersonal conflicts. *Communication Research, 9*, 201–226.

Snyder, C. R., Higgins, R. L., & Stucky, R. J. (1983). *Excuses: Masquerades in search of grace*. New York: Wiley.

Soloman, M. (1990). *Working with difficult people*. Englewood Cliffs, NJ: Prentice-Hall.

Tennen, H., & Affleck, G. (1990). Blaming others for threatening events. *Psychological Bulletin, 108*, 209–232.

Thomas, L. (1979). *The medusa and the snail*. New York: Viking Press.

Valles, P. (1992). *I love you, I hate you*. Tarrytown, NY: Triumph Books.

Weissberg, M. P. (1983). *Dangerous secrets: Maladaptive responses to stress*. New York: Norton.

Wetzler, S. (1992). Sugarcoated hostility. *Newsweek*, Oct. 12, 14.

Wile, D. B. (1988). *After the honeymoon: How conflict can improve your relationship*. New York: Wiley.

Wilmot, J. H., & Wilmot, W. W. (1978). *Interpersonal conflict*. Dubuque, IA: W. C. Brown.

Witt, D. D. (1987). A conflict theory of family violence. *Journal of Family Violence, 2*, 291–301.

Zuk, G. H. (1984). On the pathology of blaming. *International Journal of Family Therapy, 6*, 143–155.